Lucy Moore gets h
she can only see as God's sense of humour, as
her Messy Church ministry involves a lot of
travelling. Once she's arrived and recovered, her
role is to introduce people to Messy Church and
its support structures and encourage them that
they can do it too. She works within The Bible
Reading Fellowship, the home of Messy Church,
with a small team of very gifted people to make
the most of this wave of God's Spirit. Before
working full-time with Messy Church, Lucy was
a member of BRF's children's ministry team,
offering training for those wanting to bring the
Bible to life for children in churches and schools
across the UK, and using drama and storytelling
to explore the Bible with children herself.

Lucy's books include the *Messy Church* series, *The
Gospels Unplugged*, *Bethlehem Carols Unplugged*,
The Lord's Prayer Unplugged, *Colourful Creation* and
All-Age Worship, and she presents the *Messy Church*
DVD. A secondary school teacher by training, she
was a Lay Canon of Portsmouth Cathedral until
she moved dioceses, and enjoys acting, marvelling
at the alien world of her two adult children,
cheering on her husband in his work, walking
Minnie the dog and reading eclectically.

Text copyright © Lucy Moore 2016
The author asserts the moral right to be identified as the author of this work

Published by
The Bible Reading Fellowship
15 The Chambers, Vineyard
Abingdon OX14 3FE
United Kingdom
Tel: +44 (0)1865 319700
Email: enquiries@brf.org.uk
Website: www.brf.org.uk
BRF is a Registered Charity

ISBN 978 0 85746 415 6

First published 2016
10 9 8 7 6 5 4 3 2 1 0
All rights reserved

Acknowledgements
Unless otherwise stated, scripture quotations are taken from The Holy Bible, New
International Version (Anglicised edition) copyright © 1979, 1984, 2011 by Biblica. Used
by permission of Hodder & Stoughton Publishers, an Hachette UK company. All rights
reserved. 'NIV' is a registered trademark of Biblica. UK trademark number 1448790.

Cover photo: © Shutterstock

Every effort has been made to trace and contact copyright owners for material used
in this resource. We apologise for any inadvertent omissions or errors, and would ask
those concerned to contact us so that full acknowledgement can be made in the future.

A catalogue record for this book is available from the British Library

Printed and bound by CPI Group (UK) Ltd, Croydon CR0 4YY

MESSY HOSPITALITY

CHANGING COMMUNITIES THROUGH
FUN, FOOD, FRIENDSHIP AND FAITH

LUCY MOORE

Nā tō rourou, nā taku rourou ka ora ai te iwi.
'With your food basket and my food basket the people will thrive.'

MAORI PROVERB

This book is dedicated to the inspirational (and bibulous) planning team for Messy Church at St Paul's and St Mary's Bishopstoke: Clare, Lou, Lol, Anne, Wendy and Mike.

Thanks, too, to their families, especially Richard, Michael, Edward, Stephen, Philip, Jules, Noah, Dave and Andrew, and to the wider team and congregation, for the warm welcome we've enjoyed.

ACKNOWLEDGEMENTS

I owe a vast amount to Christine Pohl for her wisdom expressed in *Making Room: Rediscovering hospitality as a Christian tradition* (Eerdmans, 1999). Having wallowed in this book several years ago, it's become so much part of my thinking that many of the good ideas in my book can probably be credited to Christine.

CONTENTS

MESSY CHURCH SESSIONS ON HOSPITALITY

INTRODUCTION

WHY HOSPITALITY?

Hospitality is where it's at. Hospitality is where God's at. It's the key that opens the door to the kingdom. The more we've thought about this weird thing called hospitality, in our Messy Church team at The Bible Reading Fellowship, and the more we see churches doing it (and doing it so well!), the more convinced we're becoming that hospitality lies quietly at the heart not just of Messy Church but of the whole story of God and his people. It helps us to see the hows and whys of God working when we frame the mindblowing, multidimensional big picture of God at work in terms of ordinary hospitality. This framework informs, comforts and challenges us about huge questions like 'What is the church for?' and 'How can our little ailing, ageing church do mission and evangelism?' and 'How can we ordinary people shine a Christ-light into a dark world?' (or, perhaps more appropriately, 'How can we share that packed lunch with a hungry world?'). If we could crack hospitality, we wouldn't be fretting about church decline; we'd be fretting about what to do when too many people show up. Oh, hang on... we're doing that already.

There is a great deal of good material written on hospitality and you'll find that the book list on pages 191 and 192 makes for fruitful and far more erudite reading than my efforts here. What I want to do is not just to explore the theology of hospitality from a theoretical point of view, but also to enthuse you, as Messy Church leaders, with the belief that investing in hospitality is completely justified from a theological point of view. We can therefore joyfully hurl our Messy eggs into this basket with complete confidence that if a few of them shatter, they're the exceptions that prove the rule.

MESSY ORIGINS

Perhaps Messy Church has earned the right to bring our opinions to this discussion, given that food and hospitality are so bound up with each other, and food is so significant in Messy Church. In fact, it's rather telling that many of the synonyms of 'messy' have their roots in something edible. The word 'mess' itself came into English directly from an Old French word meaning 'a portion of food', and we still talk of an 'officers' mess' where officers eat. If you 'mess with' someone, you eat with them, so 'Don't mess with him!' is actually an order to excommunicate someone from your meal table and thus from your community. 'Hotchpotch', 'hash', 'mishmash' and 'medley' all have their roots in stews and soups and mixtures of edible things.

In the context of theology, the word 'mess' goes further back than its Old French version. It comes originally from the

Latin *missum*, meaning 'something *put* on a table': *mittere* is the word for 'to put' or 'to send'.

So 'mess' is something *put* on a table—just as animal sacrifices were placed on altars, or just as Communion bread and wine are usually placed on a table. It's also something *sent* from a kitchen—a place of provision and abundance. It's ready prepared, just as 'prepaid' grace is sent from God's abundant storehouses to us, his people, who can only receive it gratefully and enjoy it undeservedly.

The same Latin word gives us the English 'mission', of course. We ourselves, as God's people, are *put* as a living sacrifice into the world and *sent* out with God's good news to people who are hungry for it. These meanings have rich theological resonances—so, greetings from one risotto to another! Come mess with me!

Now for a Messy gallop around the roots of hospitality. Let's look at three key words: 'hospitality', 'host' and 'guest'.

- **Hospitality** comes from the Latin *hospitalitas* ('friendliness to guests'), which is related to *hospes*, meaning 'host' *or* 'guest'. A 'hospital' originally provided shelter for the needy before the word started to mean a place to heal the sick. The Latin for an inn, *hospitium*, is related to it, as is our word 'hostel'.

- **Host**, meaning someone who entertains others, is also related to the root-word *hospes*. The same word in English, but from a different Latin root, means an 'army' or 'enemy'. From a different root again, it means 'sacrifice'. Hence 'the hosts of heaven' means armies of angels, and the elevated 'host' means the consecrated bread lifted up by a priest at Holy Communion.

- **Guest** is a surprising word when we look at its roots. It comes from an ancient word meaning 'stranger' or 'enemy'.

So, lurking around the concept of hospitality is a sense of danger and antagonism, of hostility, of both guest and host taking a huge risk in asking for and offering hospitality. It carries hints of sleeping with swords drawn beside the bed, of meals offered in the teeth of hatred and ancient vendettas, and of a wilder time when the cultural rule of honour overcame common sense or individual antagonism.

Perhaps the ambivalent root of 'host', meaning both guest and host, shows us why: someone who is in the powerful position of offering hospitality at a certain time or place might, by the next year or in a different place, be in desperate need of hospitality herself. Ancient societies seem to have grasped a sense of mutuality that goes far beyond a narrow, individualistic understanding of 'myself'; it encompasses something communal that surpasses the individual and the moment. In other words, you offer hospitality today to someone you don't approve of, because one day you will need hospitality from someone who may not want to offer it to you.

STRANGERS AND CHURCHES

This hint of enmity and threat certainly echoes the way many churches feel about their established services. A church that is thinking about hospitality, in terms of doing more than just vaguely expecting new people to come one day, might well feel anxious about some of the following 'stranger or enemy' behaviours:

- Potential damage to our building ('They'll get paint on the chairs!')

- Ways of behaving that don't comply with ours ('They just don't know how to be quiet!')

- Exploitation of our resources ('They're just consumers! When are they going to start giving?')

- Mockery of our customs ('They went out for a cigarette during the song!')

Only recently, an established member of a Sunday congregation, when challenged that newcomers did not find her church a particularly welcoming place, declared, 'Of course it is' but went on to say that 'they [the newcomers] need to learn our ways if they want to stay. They need to fit in with us.' True hospitality means risk: the host opens the door to find a stranger and enemy there and *still* welcomes them in. It means a readiness to change oneself, not just to expect the outsider to conform completely to the patterns and habits of the church. It implies a level of humility and graciousness that, to be honest, is way beyond what many local congregations are prepared to exhibit.

This is why Messy Churches have needed to start not during the 'main' church service time but at a different time and day. That way, the inherited congregation isn't faced with the apparently impossible challenge of meeting Christ in the stranger at 10.30 on a Sunday morning, when everything is going 'just as we like it'. Is our attitude one of 'They need to learn our ways' or the more hospitable one of 'We welcome you and delight in you just as you are'?

OUTSIDERS AND CHURCHES

On a more fundamental level, perhaps hospitality involves considering our attitude to people who traditionally feel rejected by the church. What about our welcome when someone arrives who is a member of a different 'tribe' from our own, with very different language, relationships, clothing or behaviour? Do we expect them to fit in with us and behave as we do in as short a time as possible? What is our attitude to a child, a teenager, a single person, an elderly person, a person with disabilities, a person of a different gender or, perhaps, of no discernible gender? What do we expect of people from different races or cultures? People in relationships we find unusual? Families who are so far from the mythical 'mum, dad and 2.4 children' model that we find it hard to apply the word 'family' to them?

What if we *never* see people who are in any way different from ourselves? What if they don't even come through the door? Why don't they feel they can come that far? Is our hospitality so non-existent that it doesn't occur to them that they might be welcome?

WHAT IS JESUS' ROLE?

Don't read any further for a moment. Ah, sorry. Read this question, *then* don't read any further. What do you think: is Jesus host or guest?

(You can carry on reading now.) It's a fascinating question, isn't it? Especially given that the word 'host' now has sacramental overtones in some Christian circles. I want to wallow in this paradox for a moment because it's important to understand the dynamic dance between the roles of host and guest, roles that can be played by the church and by the families coming to Messy Church. This will be the foundation for our view and practice of hospitality in church.

A HOST AND A GUEST

Here are some traits or characteristics of a host (and I speak as one who has been blessed to encounter many marvellous hosts on my travels in the UK and overseas). Hosts have a certain wealth. They provide from a position of comparative strength. They give food, shelter and safety in their own property, according to their own means and their own house rules. They belong there; they are in possession; they have authority. They are generous, gracious and in control. They may help a guest to find a way of belonging, even temporarily, to their household. They have a dignity, a confidence and a power that comes from being in their own home.

Here are some traits of a guest (and again, my travelling role has placed me in this position many times). Guests are often—either physically, spiritually or emotionally—travellers. They don't belong to the community where they find themselves. They have no rights, and they have few possessions: they may be carrying their world in a suitcase or backpack. They may not speak the local language or they may be voiceless for other reasons; they may not know the rules. They may never have encountered this sort of house, bed or food before. They are vulnerable and dependent, in a position of needing to receive. They are aliens with a history that no one there knows, far from any place, people or possessions that help them feel at home. Sojourning and being temporary are all elements of being a guest.

HOSPITALITY IN THE BIBLE

The virtue of hospitality is a thread running brightly through the Old and New Testaments. There isn't space here to explore the strong theme of what 'home' itself means as a reality and as a symbol in the Bible, but underlying our understanding of hospitality should be the ancient understanding of God's people as 'strangers and sojourners' (see, for example, Psalm 39:12, KJV) rather than people who are completely at home on earth. This idea is found all the way through the Bible, from the moment when Adam and Eve leave Eden. The acceptance that we're only here on a temporary basis affects our view of 'our' belongings, 'our' homes and 'our' status. It's paradoxical, because we're also called to be firmly contextualised and to minister where God has placed us. We need to feel completely 'at home' where God has placed us while knowing that it's not our ultimate home. (As an aside, this might mean deciding to get involved with an 'ordinary' local church, rather than travelling long distances to find one which seems to boast more exciting children's work, teaching or sung worship. Perhaps we can take on the responsibility to change things for the better, where we are.)

I've written elsewhere (in *Messy Church 2*) about the glorious story from Genesis 18 of Abraham and the three strangers, which still stands as an archetypal example of the way a community expressing generous hospitality can expect to receive unimaginable blessing, a hope and a future. For many churches who have lost touch with any children or young people over the last 70 years or so, it's a story that offers hope particularly through the coming of a child, Isaac, into a previously barren relationship. We rejoice that so many Messy Churches are throwing open their camps, as Abraham and Sarah did, to the strangers in the desert of their communities. These churches give of their best to the strangers, at great personal cost, and in return are slowly (or, by God's grace, speedily) receiving the blessing of a new congregation of children, young people and older ones. They are seeing a hope and a future where once there was no prospect of anything but dwindling and death. This is the power of hospitality.

HOSPITALITY SOURED

Uncomfortably (and when are we ever encouraged to stay comfortable for long?) close to the story of the three strangers is the grim counterpoint in the story of Sodom, where we see the evils of hospitality gone wrong (Genesis 19). This is echoed later, as a sign that the people of God have reached absolute rock bottom, in the horrific account of the gang rape of the concubine in Judges 19. The latter is a shockingly vivid story. It tells first of the joyful reconciliatory hospitality shown by the concubine's father (vv. 3–9) and the more anxious but still generous hospitality of an old man in Gibeah (vv. 16–21). But these examples contrast with the appalling behaviour of those who should also act as hosts in Gibeah but instead betray every precept of hospitality and decency. They force the old man into an impossible situation and the concubine, the most vulnerable member of the household, is found, poignantly, 'fallen in the doorway of the house, with her hands on the threshold' (v. 27). If we need any further indication that a betrayal of hospitality is a universal sign of godlessness that cannot be ignored, and that hospitality is vital if God's unnamed little people are to be protected, we see the result of this atrocity—brutal civil war and unbearable suffering and the final despairing words of Judges, 'In those days Israel had no king; everyone did as they saw fit' (21:25). Good hospitality—unobtrusively working in the background as a 'given', not as an exception—is a sign of society functioning in a godly way. For us, in a post-resurrection world, it is a sign of the kingdom and the means by which we can grow the kingdom.

HOSPITALITY IN THE PARABLES OF JESUS

We'll come to the accounts of Jesus in the Gospels in a minute, but let's first think of Jesus' parables. How can we understand hospitality from them? See how often a window on hospitality is opened through these punchy stories. In the parable of the good Samaritan (Luke 10:25–37), the man from Samaria pays for hospitality for the injured traveller and opens himself to vulnerability on the road too, by stopping to help. In the parable of the prodigal son (Luke 15:11–32), the father welcomes his wayward son home by dressing him in fine clothes and throwing a party in his honour. The parable of the great banquet (Matthew 22:1–14) hints that Jesus understands the kingdom to be something like a wedding party with an etiquette and a dress code, where the host is very firmly in control and sets his own (somewhat draconian) house rules for the guests. Similarly, the story of the workers in the vineyard (Matthew 20:1–15) shows a 'host' who is determined to run his household business in the way he wants, not influenced by what the prevailing culture says he should do (here expressed in terms of payment). The parable of the mustard seed (Matthew 13:31–32) features birds—those garden pests—finding hospitality, sanctuary and shelter in the branches of the mustard bush. The parable of the sheep and the goats (Matthew 25:31–46) shows clearly that the welcome we give to the vulnerable people around us is taken as something of great heavenly significance in the currency of the kingdom.

Hospitality runs through these stories as a godly, wholesome thread, as evidence of kingdom life. Jesus knew how central it is to our attitudes and to the way we live our lives on God's planet.

HOSPITALITY IN THE EARLY CHURCH

In the New Testament epistles, we see the writers encouraging the new church to be hospitable to its own members and to the needy. The 17th-century poet and preacher John Donne was very forthright about the New Testament concept of hospitality and characteristically colourful in his explanation of it. He thought these passages actually meant that the church should be hospitable only to its scattered members who had suffered persecution, rather than to outsiders like those of Donne's own day: 'Those vagabonds and incorrigible rogues that fill porches and barns in this country, a very great part of them was never baptised: people of a promiscuous generation and a mischievous education; ill brought into the world and never brought into the church' (Sermon XL). Indeed, some of the biblical letters do seem to be focused on the extended church rather than looking outwards: see 1 Peter 4:9, 'Offer hospitality to one another without grumbling'; 3 John 1:8, 'We ought therefore to show hospitality to such people so that we may work together for the truth'; and Romans 12:13, 'Share with God's people who are in need. Practise hospitality.'

Hurrah for Lydia (Acts 16:13–15), Publius (Acts 28:7–10), Gaius (Romans 16:23) and others who provided hospitality so that the gospel could be not only shared but also demonstrated throughout the Mediterranean region. Our churches should be communities where we are welcomed into each other's homes, where hospitality is a pleasure to offer and to receive, a mark of who we are. Hurrah, too, for the massive teams under Stephen and his friends who provided hospitality on a vast scale to the needy, with the energy and passion of the very early church in Acts 6:1–7; hurrah for the cheery women in 1 Timothy 5:10 who quietly provided hospitality to those in need as a habit of life, a deep character trait, a joy rather than a burden.

The admonition of Hebrews 13:2 goes to the very heart and soul of hospitality, to the sheep-and-goats parable of Jesus and the mystery of faith: 'Do not forget to show hospitality to strangers, for by so doing some people have shown hospitality to angels without knowing it.' We probably only get to show hospitality to one angel for (what do you think?) every 500 or so human beings, so perhaps we'd better get on with being hospitable to strangers in our churches, homes, workplaces and schools, and in our every conversation or chance encounter, to increase our chances of meeting an angelic visitor every now and then!

SO IS JESUS HOST OR GUEST?

We've already glanced at the Latin roots for hospitality-related words. However, the Greek word for 'guest', 'host' *and* 'stranger' is *xenos*. 'The semantic fluidity conveys the blurred identities of guest and host heightened by the recognition of Christ,' writes Amy Oden in *Ancient and Postmodern Christianity: Paleo-orthodoxy in the 21st century* (edited by Christopher Hall and Kenneth Tanner, IVP, 2002). Think about the famous description of Jesus that Paul gives in Philippians 2:6–11, in the context of working out how to treat each other in a Christian community. You will know it off by heart and can check it in a Bible, so here's a paraphrase I've written especially for Messy Church teams:

Go back to Jesus as the shining example, who let go of everything—status, respect, reputation, wealth, time, space, cleanness, tidiness, oversight, authority, power, predictability, what he had always done, where he always sat—and went on an adventure. He swapped all those things for messiness, dirt, betrayal, unpredictability, cost, pain, isolation, vulnerability, puzzlement, despair, suffering, danger, right through to death itself. But look at the payback! This was the only way to turn heaven and earth upside down and kick off the new age of the kingdom, where everyone and anyone can know how glorious Jesus really is and can get a glimpse of his glorious reality and start to help put things right. We can do no better than worship our glorious, vindicated, resurrected, successful, Gold Medal Jesus.

Jesus was the ultimate host. He had so much; he was so powerful. He was the Creator, the author of the universe, the one enthroned way above the earth, protected, protecting, providing and powerful, totally at home in a setting worthy of his awesomeness. Of the two descriptions, 'host' and 'guest', Jesus was the host *par excellence*. But he was so sure of who he was and what his calling was—his identity and his role—that he could let go of everything and turn willingly from host to guest, becoming entirely vulnerable, dependent and needy. He became a baby, utterly reliant on the gracious hosting of a mother's body and then his parents' care. The safe home in Bethlehem became a death trap, so he had to become that most needy of guests, a refugee, in Egypt. When he might have settled into a safe home life, he abandoned Nazareth for the wilderness, for three years of homelessness, depending on God and on the hospitality of others. He let go of more and more, until he let go even of the 'home' he'd been living in for 33 years—his actual body. This was vulnerability at its most extreme. This was where the host, planet Earth, broke all the rules of hospitality and slaughtered the guest—the enemy—in his time of apparent weakness. It was the ultimate betrayal.

Jesus became this needy guest and, knowing what would happen, still went through with it because of love. This love can now welcome his previous enemies in through the wide open door of his heavenly kingdom and invite them to feast at his table.

Even more exciting than this framing of Jesus' entire life as the host who became a guest, though, is the way he lived his life during the three years we know most about. Jesus spent these years of his adult life seeming to swap deliberately between the roles of guest and host, subverting what people assume to be the rights and wrongs of hospitality. There are so many examples, so where do we start?

HOSPITALITY IN THE GOSPELS

Let's put the obvious one out on the table: Jesus chose deliberately to spend much of his time eating at the houses of people whom everyone else considered to be nasty bits of work. He was criticised for it; his reputation was at risk because of it; he presumably had to cope with a lot of unsuitable language and inappropriate behaviour that might have made him uncomfortable and deeply sad for those involved. But he carried on eating with those people.

Might Jesus actually have preferred their honestly upfront bad behaviour to the hypocrisy and machinations of the religious elite? Maybe eating with the tax collectors wasn't a penance to him, but a privilege, as they invited him into their homes and conversations, shared their hopes and fears, and contrasted their life choices with those of this warm, gentle, tough, honest young rabbi enjoying their goat stew. The Pharisees (unlike some religious communities, such as the Essenes) chose to live among 'ordinary' people, not safely isolated from contamination. But, to preserve their 'holiness', the one thing the Pharisees would not do was to eat with people who weren't themselves Pharisees: this was a mark of their distinctiveness. No wonder Jesus shocked them by the people he ate with!

Jesus seems to have had an unusual view of hospitality—of who is the owner of a home and even of what 'home' means. Think about the visit to Jerusalem when he was twelve: 'Didn't you know I had to be in my Father's house?' he asks his relieved parents when they eventually catch up with him (Luke 2:49). He seems to ask it with genuine bewilderment, as if he knows already that the home in Nazareth is only one sort of home and that his own concept of 'home' is multidimensional.

Look at Martha and Mary, in Luke 10:38–42. There's no doubt that Jesus and his disciples are the guests and Martha and Mary are the hosts. But when Mary breaks the rules of gender and hospitality and sits—like a man and like a guest—at Jesus' feet instead of providing food as a hostess should, Jesus says that she has chosen a better way than

Martha, who is busy hostessing for all she's worth. Is Jesus the guest in this instance or is he the host, destroying and recreating the household rules?

The story of Zacchaeus in Luke 19:1–9 is a telling one. Who is the host and who is the guest here? Surely a host should make the invitation and the guest should receive it? But instead we see Jesus inviting himself (and presumably his disciples) to Zacchaeus' house, and Zacchaeus receiving far more from Jesus than Jesus receives from him. Jesus is the provider and makes a way, through his acceptance of this sinner's 'unclean' hospitality, for Zacchaeus to re-enter his community, this time as a provider himself rather than a parasite. Zacchaeus' whole view of what is valuable is turned upside down by Jesus' visit.

At the feeding of the 5000, who are the hosts and who are the guests? '*You* give them something to eat,' says Jesus to the disciples, as if he wants them to take on the role of host while he sits back and picnics (Luke 9:13), but they can't see that they have the equipment, the facilities. They're not at home out in the wilderness. It isn't where they belong. They have nothing to give; they see themselves as vulnerable guests. It's an outsider, a small boy who isn't even named (John 6:9), who gets the joke and provides the impossibly small amount because, in the true spirit of hospitality, that's everything he has. So, the child becomes host to 5000 people. This is a comical, shocking, upside-down situation: the powerful male adults' powerlessness and over-intellectualisation ('Rationally, *obviously* we have nothing to give') are thrown into sharp relief by the boy's spontaneous, instinctive hospitality, which is blessed by Jesus and turned into a glorious demonstration of kingdom hospitality by his own hospitable power. Christ turns even the wildest desert into a welcoming and hospitable home.

At Simon the Pharisee's house in Luke 7:36–50, Jesus challenges the assumption that Simon is the host in his own house when a total outsider—the woman with the perfume—behaves more like a good, welcoming host than Simon has done.

At the last supper, the paradox is taken even further when the host becomes the slave and washes his guests' feet, taking on the most abject role at the meal to the horror of his guests (John 13:1–7). This is role reversal of a very uncomfortable nature—embarrassing, shocking, creepy, frankly weird. This is not what the head of a household does; it is not what a host does. The guests are disturbed to their very core: this is not the welcome they expected or wanted. The rules are being subverted. Then, the unpredictable, rule-breaking host not only provides the food but becomes the food (Matthew 26:26). Hospitality becomes a giving, not merely of what he has but of who he is.

On the road to Emmaus (Luke 24:13–35), the disciples invite Jesus in to eat with them as their guest, but it is Jesus who, like a host, takes the bread and breaks it. It is he who provides for them, in food that goes far beyond bread alone, through the conversation on the way to the meal.

At the breakfast on the beach in John 21:4–13, Jesus has made a fire and provided some of the food, but he invites the disciples to bring the fish they've just caught too. A host who encourages guests to contribute to the table? Bring and share? What is he trying to demonstrate? Is he saying that, like the boy with the packed lunch in John 6, the disciples will always have something of their own to bring to the table? Is he trying to show a kingdom pattern—that the supernatural will be provided free of charge but, in the work of God, human beings should bring what they can of their natural resources too? 'Bring some of the fish you have just caught' (v. 10). Jesus, as host, has so little need to prove himself that he makes space for guests to give as well as receive: they all have something to offer that will be needed for a complete and perfect experience.

It's probably justifiable to culminate with the comforting and challenging words of Revelation 3:20: 'Here I am! I stand at the door and knock. If anyone hears my voice and opens the door, I will come in and eat with that person, and they with me.' A guest stands at a door and knocks. Even after Jesus has proved his glorious identity, power and authority by dying and rising to new life, he is still willing to take the humble, courteous role of a guest when he comes to each person. He is someone to sit and enjoy a meal with, a welcome guest, one who honours us and whom we honour in return. We'd be thrilled if he only favoured a Tweet we'd posted—and here he is with his feet under the table in our kitchen! He challenges us as churches and as individuals, by his bold and fearless door-knocking, to be outgoing and confident. He challenges us, in his humility, to be as courteous and gracious as he is, to receive as well as to give.

CHURCH AS HOST OR GUEST: DELIGHTS AND DANGERS

Maybe Jesus is demonstrating that, in the dance between God and human beings, it's only God who is the ultimate host and the ultimate guest. We, as individuals or as church, should always be in the crossover place, being great hosts *and* great guests in our dealings with each other and with the world around us. We see this interplay through the overarching mission of Jesus that Paul describes in Philippians 2:6–11, and in Jesus' everyday interactions with the people he encountered throughout his life. The church can never sit firmly as unequivocal host or unequivocal guest, but is called to waltz happily from one role to the other, just as Jesus modelled.

In our personal walk with God, we will be called sometimes to be generous hosts and sometimes to be vulnerable guests. It's not our church; it's God's. We do not hold the power and authority over its house rules; he does. We are all his guests, from the oldest, most generous person on the planned giving scheme to the newest, youngest, most demanding person who toddles into the circle. Nor are we merely guests who simply slob around the table, ignore the washing-up, watch the minister run herself ragged, snore the afternoon away and complain, 'This church doesn't *feed* me…' We are all hosts, there to provide for each other and for those who haven't yet found their way in to the table.

A church is called to join in this understanding of itself in a dynamic, ever-changing dance from host to guest, and from guest to host. We are invited to a banquet and given not just more food than we can see, let alone eat, but a tea towel. As soon as we lay the table, God places food on it. We put on our Messy aprons to serve but find ourselves seated behind a plate of pasta to eat. As soon as we sit down to eat, we are called to wait on others. As we serve others, we find that our plate has been filled fuller than it was before. As we have more on our plate, we have more to give out and more enthusiasm about helping others to taste and see this miracle for themselves.

In churches, there is a danger that we will arrogantly see ourselves as the host with everything to give and nothing to take. 'We have the words of eternal life; we have all the answers; we have no need of anyone else but they need us desperately. We can pass our bounty on to those needy people outside. We have nothing to do but give; they can only take.' This is one mistake. Instead, we need to be continually searching for a healthy balance between knowing our identity—having a superstrong core understanding of what this church in this place at this season is and does—and listening to God, to the outsider and to each other. We need to perceive where we need to change and grow, what habits we've developed that are offputting for others ('That's *my* pew, thank you very much'), and which traditions were only for decoration, or were necessary for a particular time and are now getting in the way of God's work in our community. Like hospitality itself, this takes wisdom, humility, energy and sacrifice. It means that church won't be me-centred but will offer a painful example of taking up our cross and following Jesus. Like Paul's plea in Philippians 2:3, it means 'considering others better than ourselves'—especially when we're sure they are *not* better than us!

It's tough, isn't it, this hospitality stuff? Look how quickly a commitment to hospitality turns into suffering, sacrifice and dying to live. Maybe something as bouncy as Messy Church should have left this tough business to traditional church and just messed about on the edges, having fun. But no—from the start, hospitality has been at the heart of what Messy Church is. The more we do it with conviction, as a church community and as individuals and families, the more joy and freedom we and others will find in discovering the heart of our hospitable God.

But there's more! Another way for a host household to miss the point is to be entirely self-sufficient—so efficient that it needs no additions from outside. Indeed, any additions would actually get in the way of the smooth operation of the household. 'We have people to do all the jobs. We don't need anyone else. Others would get in the way; they wouldn't do it right; they wouldn't do it as professionally as we do it.'

This is a massive risk run by all churches, including Messy Churches. Only recently, at our planning meeting, one team member bewailed the fact that we can't get enough people from our existing Sunday congregations to run Messy Church: 'It's a poor show, if these are all the people prepared to help…!' It's true in one sense but it's also given us the opportunity to take up offers of help from the new families and ask them to lead an activity table. (And they said yes!) If our team was complete, we wouldn't have space to include them. Perhaps (*perhaps!*) the ready-made Christians would do a better job, know the story better, or be more professional. But what matters most—a professional, slick operation or a mutually giving and taking, sending and receiving community, where nothing is so perfect that it seems unattainable except by the holy few? And when do people start growing as disciples? Sometimes it's when they start leading or giving, rather than just receiving; when they understand themselves as hosts as well as guests.

Another danger we can see from the image of hosts and guests is that we might be a host who encourages half the household to sit back, surrounded by chocolate, while the other half works itself to the bone. This is the reality, of course. We know that any church—indeed, any organisation—will include some people who do more than others. This might be because of changing circumstances: I find it a lot easier to commit to activities involving going out in the evening, now that my children don't need babysitters, and I can do more than I could at the time when my back was in spasm or when my extended farflung family members needed more of my time. One day I'll be in a better position to commit to regular weekly events, when the current season of travelling and strange working hours is over (when I'm about 90, probably). But it's frustrating when an inherited church congregation leaves a Messy Church to be run by a handful of people and comes up with excuses like 'I've done my bit; it's down to the young ones now' or 'I don't have time.' No time even to make a cake? To pray? To come and set up the tables or clear them away afterwards? To ask how things went last time?

I don't buy the 'no time' argument. We make time for what we want to make time for, and our commitment to Jesus shows in our use of time. 'I have no calling to this ministry': isn't that more the issue? Some of the people behaving like guests in our churches need to be energised to see themselves as hosts, to become crew members instead of cruise passengers.

Another, more extreme temptation for a church might be to manipulate the stranger to fit a mould, like a sanitised version of the villain Procrustes in the Theseus myth. (He welcomed in travellers, then strapped them to a bed, chopping off bits from anyone who was too tall and stretching out on a rack anyone who was too short. Those Greeks knew how to party!) Here, the host is all-powerful and transforms lives, but with no sense that there are any ways of being human other than the single, predefined way that suits them. A guest in this setting would be well advised to run for the hills before they're damaged beyond repair.

There are dangers inherent in being a church that sees itself as a guest, too—perhaps a guest who just takes from richer hosts. This kind of church may be happy to have a minister and a building provided by the district or diocese or other denominational structure, but is not prepared to contribute anything or to join in the networks provided by the structure. It sees no need to listen to any hint that it should effect change in itself or others. A permanent guest is a burden to its host and needs to be challenged to contribute to the household or to move on.

Guests can also threaten the stable running of a household by putting an overwhelming strain on the host. In *Making Room: Rediscovering hospitality as a Christian virtue* (Eerdmans, 1999), Christine Pohl studies different hospitable Christian communities and makes it clear that the host needs to work out how to protect its own identity, especially if it is practising radical hospitality among those who are so damaged that they are prone to exploit and harm the host.

As churches, we need to keep the confidence and gracious resources of the good host balanced with the openness, gratitude and respect of the good guest. We need to be generous but willing to learn and change. We need to be open to receive as well as to give, to be changed ourselves as well as to help change others.

SYSTEMATIC HOSPITALITY

The monasteries were the first Christian places to attempt a systematic way of welcoming vulnerable travellers. St Benedict wrote about this, particularly in Rule 53, which happily blends a cosmic overview with the practical protection of the order and identity of the monastery, so that the arrival of guests doesn't throw the host into disarray. On the one hand, he writes, 'In the reception of the poor and of pilgrims the greatest care and solicitude should be shown, because it is especially in them that Christ is received,' while on the other, he advocates a separate kitchen for guests, 'that the brethren may not be disturbed when guests, who are never lacking in a monastery, arrive at irregular hours'. It was through the monasteries that offshoots of hospitality, such as hospitals and schools, became established, too. But where monasteries later went wrong was perhaps in turning the open-handed welcome that Benedict advocated, with its bias towards the poor and needy, into a system for gaining favour with people of influence so that those people would give back financial support to the monastery. Their hospitality lost its heart and became a means of manipulation: rich people became more welcome than poor people.

In our own day, hospitality (like schools and hospitals) has been taken over by government and industry. Do an internet search for 'hospitality' and you will almost certainly find hospitality careers, corporate hospitality, the hotel industry and restaurant businesses before you find any mention of the church. Yet hospitality has remained a constant pulse, beating fiercely or gently in the church, to present times.

Recently, churches, monastic communities and inspired individuals have been quietly demonstrating for us what hospitality in the 21st century looks like. L'Arche is a shining example. New monasticism is working at it. Christian communities such as Urban Vision in New Zealand (www. urbanvision.org.nz) practise it sacrificially. How about this for the first 'texture' on Urban Vision's website to describe what they do: 'We are generous with our homes, our mealtimes, our bedspaces, our personal wealth, our emotional energy, and our time. Embracing and including the "other" is important to us.' Hospitality is in the very lifeblood of communities like Hilfield Friary in Dorset. Alpha works through it. Foodbanks are a vibrant expression of it. It is also our joy, privilege and priority in Messy Church.

There is a tension, still, between hospitality for the sheer joy and love of others and hospitality as a means to evangelise. My sense is that we shouldn't fall into the trap of using hospitality as a means to an end, but should exercise it out of love, expecting God to bless us through it. We are hospitable because that is who we are; it is an expression of our love of God and neighbour. We are not hospitable because it's a good evangelistic tool. God can and does look after that side-effect of hospitality.

THE WONDERS OF HOSPITALITY

I want to have written the following, but I didn't.

Hospitality is not to change people, but to offer them space where change can take place. It is not to bring men and women over to our side, but to offer freedom not disturbed by dividing lines. It is not to lead our neighbour into a corner where there are no alternatives left, but to open a wide spectrum of options for choice and commitment. It is not an educated intimidation with good books, good stories, and good works, but the liberation of fearful hearts so that words can find roots and bear ample fruit... The paradox of hospitality is that it wants to create emptiness, not a fearful emptiness, but a friendly emptiness where strangers can enter and discover themselves as created free... not a subtle invitation to adopt the lifestyle of the host, but the gift of a chance for the guest to find his own.
HENRI J.M. NOUWEN, *REACHING OUT: THE THREE MOVEMENTS OF THE SPIRITUAL LIFE* (BANTAM DOUBLEDAY DELL, 2000)

It's great, isn't it? The website of the Order of St Benedict, too, phrases its expression of hospitality beautifully:

Contemporary monasticism in North America and elsewhere is coming to understand that the greatest gift monastics can offer the contemporary world is a place where people live a balanced life, a place where peace is the quest and aim (Rule of Benedict Prol. 17), a place not so interested in going out to save the world but in letting the world experience the salvation already won in Christ Jesus, a place where all are guests, even the monastics, in the house of God, respecting and cherishing one another, a place where hearts overflow 'with the inexpressible delight of love' (Rule of Benedict Prol. 49).

WWW.OSB.ORG/ABA/LAW/MLL12.HTM

In new monasticism, hospitality is described as a tradition to maintain: 'Radical hospitality, allowing people to belong to the community, participating in its life and then being able to explore the Christian faith… is faithful to the ongoing monastic tradition' (Ian Mobsby and Mark Berry, *A New Monastic Handbook*, Canterbury Press, 2014, p. 23).

One of the exciting outcomes of Messy Church is that ordinary local churches are enabled to express their passion for welcoming the poor and the pilgrim into the church community (and often the building) that they love and want to share. Until now they may have found it hard to get people to want to come through the door, but Messy Church gives their hospitable instincts a framework within which to demonstrate the open-handed, open-hearted welcome to others that Christ has already extended to them.

HOSPITABLE GOD

Heaven is our ultimate home. Our en-suite penthouse there is reserved and paid for and we have the reservation safe in our pocket through the indwelling of the Holy Spirit. We're walking (some of us might be quadbiking, microlighting, rollerblading, being driven in an open carriage behind six plumed horses, or at the wheel of a Lamborghini) down the drive already and enjoying the landscaped gardens and the view of the stately home towards which we're heading. The Lord of the Manor who met us at the gate is travelling alongside us whenever he can, or just leaving us free to find our own path. On the way, we're showing everyone else how to get to and around this wonderful estate—giving them fruit out of its greenhouses, taking selfies with them as we have fun in its adventure playground, tweeting about our explorations of the walled garden, Facebooking our foray into the vibrant workshops, getting muddy in the sunshine while clearing out the lake, pointing out signposts and making paths across wildernesses in case our friends want to come here too. It's not *our* home. It doesn't belong to us (how on earth could we afford it?). But it's a place where we are welcomed by name and with a great party, as if the host had been waiting all his life for us to arrive—as indeed he has.

QUESTIONS

- 'Hospitality becomes a giving, not merely of what he (Jesus at the last supper) has but of who he is.' Is there a danger that we offer things, but not ourselves, to outsiders?

- 'We probably only get to show hospitality to one angel for (what do you think?) every 500 or so human beings, so perhaps we'd better get on with being hospitable to strangers in our churches, homes, workplaces and schools, and in our every conversation or chance encounter, to increase our chances of meeting an angelic visitor every now and then!' How exactly can we be hospitable in these different environments?

- How willing are we to ask for help from the stranger? Why might we be reluctant to give them a chance to demonstrate hospitality to us?

- How much do you think the hospitality of a church reflects its stance on holding on to or releasing power?

CHAPTER 1

HOSPITALITY AT THE WELCOME TABLE

In the next four chapters we drill down into the detail of the four 'tables' of Messy Church—the welcome, the activities, the celebration and the meal—to see how we can make the most of the opportunities that each of them gives to demonstrate Christ's open-handed and openhearted hospitality. Many of the practical suggestions can be found elsewhere in the Messy Church resources, but, viewed through the lens of hospitality, they may be seen as more significant than just 'common sense' or 'a good idea'.

THE WELCOME TIME

I once went to a church on a Sunday. The heavy wooden door was closed and there was no sign of life outside it.

I was five or ten minutes early for the start time of the service. I put my hand on the door handle, wondering if

I should push or pull, wondering if it was locked anyway and if I would just look a wee bit silly for even trying it. But I'm a grown-up! I've travelled three continents! I've been a Christian all my life! I can *do* this thing! The door opened (oh joy, oh miraculous relief, thank you, Lord) and I walked in, closing it carefully behind me, ready for the next people to worry about.

Two people were busy sorting out the coffee by the door—not serving any, just getting organised. Several people were already sitting in the chairs, ready for the service, with their backs to me. There was a pile of books and papers on a small table nearby that looked like the sort of kit you need for a service. Was this what was needed for today? Or would it all be on the screen? One of the coffee people half turned and half smiled, then turned back to her conversation. I reached out my hand towards the books. Someone materialised, hovering protectively over them, and I snatched my hand back, like a shoplifter caught in the act. She stared at something beyond my shoulder and wordlessly held out a handful of books and fliers. I walked on past another couple of half-smiles that obviously interrupted more important conversations and pre-service jobs. I looked in mild panic at the choice of seats. Some had hassocks on: was this the local equivalent of staking your claim to a sunbed with your towel? Some had people sitting in them, staring at their feet or straight ahead, or deep in conversation with each other. Fortunately, I *didn't* make for one particular set of seats. This, I later discovered from a friend who had made the mistake on her first visit, was Where Some People Always Sat. Had I sat in them, I was told, there would have been very English, very nonconfrontational but oh-so-coercive, almost inaudible but just audible enough mutterings about the true and established ownership of those seats—until I would have felt compelled to 'move lower down, my friend'.

I sat and peered round to check what I should be doing. The minister, arriving in a swoosh of robes, passed us, noticed me, paused in his rush to the vestry, smiled warmly and welcomed me as if he was delighted I was there, before dashing off to get the service started. And so we began.

This is not much of a story, is it? It's not terribly funny or memorable. Nobody was aggressive. I didn't run away from the church screaming, 'Anathema! Never again!' There was nothing that left the other members of the congregation shocked or appalled or calling for change. They didn't even notice. But if I hadn't been a Christian already, and one who feels quite passionately that Christians should be at their local church unless God has explicitly invited them to go elsewhere; if I hadn't got a bloodyminded streak in me that tells me no church is perfect and sometimes you have to change things from the inside; if it hadn't been for the minister and his wife who chatted to me after the service as well… would I have gone back? I think not. Yet this is a church that describes itself as 'very welcoming'. Frankly, nobody in it that day, with those two honourable exceptions, demonstrated welcome. The defensive cry of 'We're very welcoming!' sounds like someone in a doctor's surgery crying, 'I'm fit as a fiddle!' when their skin's gone green, one arm's fallen off and there's an axe stuck in their skull. Saying, 'But we're a very welcoming church' just means we never do anything about the fact that we're not—we're *really* not. A vague smile from a distance does not make anyone welcome, however much it cost the person smiling. A person handing out books is not some insignificant jobsworth who can do their job as grumpily as they want, but a Peter entrusted with the keys to heaven, the first indication of what sort of a church this is. For us on the visit above, she was more of a Gandalf, faced with us, the Balrog, on the Bridge of Khazad-dum: 'YOU SHALL NOT PASS.'

The way we meet people at the door is merely the trivial froth of hospitality in the life of a church. It's a tiny symbolic fraction of our character as a church community, of our deep-seated attitude to outsiders, of our opinion of ourselves and our rights. This is why we need to understand that it's not our church; it's God's. He is the host, and we are *all* guests. We need to interact with those around us from a position of humility, not arrogance.

Paradoxically, it's why we need to understand our role also as hosts on Christ's behalf, and carry it out with confidence, a strong sense of identity, and joy. The 'greeting at the door' is only cosmetic and can be easily changed with a smattering of training and self-awareness, but the attitude that the 'greeting at the door' symbolises is far harder to change, because true welcome goes far deeper than bouncing around at the door of a church once a week. It is about a whole-of-life discipleship that welcomes Christ in the stranger, seven days a week, in buildings and settings far beyond the church building. It means delighting in and loving those who are different from us, and sharing power with them. It goes way beyond the tolerance that you can find in any public amenity, like a gym or a community group, provoking the comment 'See how they love each other!' It marks us as either an inward-looking or an outward-looking church.

How can our Messy Churches make sure that what people experience is not the socially acceptable, bland accessibility that they can find in a department store or a chain of restaurants anywhere in the country, but instead the glorious welcome of the Lord of hosts himself?

There is at least one liberating factor: Messy Church is so new that we *can* do things differently from how they've always been done, with teams who believe in mission, are outward-looking by nature and are coming to church to serve others, not themselves. We are not tied by the need not to hurt Mr X's feelings by taking him off the welcome team when he's been on it for the last 300 years. We can (and should) keep doing things differently, partly to keep them fresh and effective in a rapidly changing world and partly so that we don't fall into the trap of saying, 'We do this in Messy Church because we've *always* done it in Messy Church.' As with everything in Messy Church, the high-minded 'view from the top of the mountain'—our theology and our ecclesiology—is expressed in the down-to-earth details of practicalities. We proclaim the trinitarian, relational God who, by grace, welcomes us into his kingdom, in part by having clean toilets. (Or perhaps it would be more accurate to say that our proclamation of our God is not revealed to be hypocritical and empty because we couldn't be bothered to check the state of the toilets.) So this chapter is very down to earth.

Many Messy Churches find that they have new people coming each time. This means we can never sit back and assume that everyone knows what to do, where to go and what time things will happen. A hospitable welcome will always be a necessary ministry within it.

One of the vital aspects of being a fresh expression of church is the need for three-dimensional listening—listening to God, to each other and to the community we are trying to serve. In a Messy Church context, this listening is a way of expressing our commitment to hospitality. A good host looks to the needs of the guests as well as to his or her own needs. In a Christian community, there is always a balance to be held, as Benedict discovered, between the needs of the church team and the needs of the Messy congregation; otherwise the outsiders might overwhelm the hosts and destroy the very identity that makes it possible for them to be hospitable. But the humility of a good host is shown partly in the refusal to say, 'We've got all the answers and you guests need to learn from us and behave like us'; instead, we should be always looking out for Christ in the stranger, and for the wisdom and insight brought by the youngest, oldest or least able person. We need to be looking out for the way *we* need to change through *them*.

In 2015, the Consultative Group for Ministry among Children (CGMC) drew up this checklist for any church wanting to welcome people of all generations.

1. Include children and young people on the welcome team.

2. Make sure the welcomers know that the welcome is for everyone.

3. Have many thresholds of welcome throughout the whole service.

4. Don't assume that people know what's going on; explain everything that is happening.

5. Beware being patronising.

6. Engage with people's real life stories.

7. Make sure that any talking from the front is intentionally addressed to everyone.

8. Recognise that worship is 'the work of the people' (the root meaning of 'liturgy') and goes beyond the service time limits.

9. Aim to make your worship a multi-voiced gathering, open to all.

10. Make sure the going out from your worship is also a good experience.

Which of these does your church already do well? Which of the others would be practical to implement?

HOSPITABLE PREPARATION

Ask yourself these questions.

- Is your Messy Church being held on a day that suits (enough) local families or on a day that is convenient for the church?

- Have you hospitably considered other churches in the area and invited them to join you in this mission, or considered joining them in theirs?

- Is Messy Church being held in the building that is most appropriate for your guests or easiest for your church?

- Are there any ways you need to contextualise the Messy Church framework to make it appropriate for your particular setting and the families you're trying to reach?

- How might/do you ask for feedback from the families coming and act on their suggestions?

The next part of hospitality is signposting people towards Messy Church through invitation and publicity. Again, here are some questions to ask.

- Do we need to review our posters, banners and fliers?

- Have we checked out the options for Messy Church poster designs on www.cpo-online.org.uk?

- Has anyone checked our web publicity recently? Is the information on the church website or Facebook page up to date?

- Is our publicity design and content welcoming to all ages, genders and socio-economic groups? Is it welcoming to single people and families?

- Is the publicity going out to strategic places?

- Are we equipping our Sunday church members and Messy Church members with publicity materials to hand out to their friends?

- Are our Twitter-friendly church members prepared to tweet about it?

ARRIVING AT MESSY CHURCH

It's hard to overestimate how crucial the initial welcome is, in a society that is pretty hostile to the church and other faith communities. Our hospitality needs to shine through and take people by surprise from the moment they walk through the door. A welcomer's job isn't to get the family's name on the register; it's to be the prodigal son's father, delighted to see his son coming home. You may not feel it appropriate to rush down the road towards them, fling your arms round them, holler for jewellery and clean clothes and slaughter the nearest cow, but the celebratory, all-accepting, unshockable glory of your welcome to each and every person should recall the father's attitude (and when you get round to telling that parable, it will make complete sense to the families you've welcomed). You're not simply seeing a family coming to church; you're seeing the lost sheep being carried out of danger, the Israelites arriving in the promised land, the gates of hell crumbling; you're seeing your long-lost brother and sister coming home. No wonder they get a warm welcome!

Here are some questions to consider.

- A team exercise: on your own, go to a community gathering or facility that you've never entered before—a meeting, a choir, a club, a pub, a nail bar, a betting shop or a bingo hall. (Going to another church is cheating, although it can be eye-opening.) Come back and tell the rest of the team how you felt and what made you feel welcome or unwelcome. What changes can you make from these insights that will benefit your Messy Church?

- Stand together in your entrance and talk about the impression it gives. As people arrive at your Messy Church, is the physical entrance as welcoming as it could be?

- Does anything need sorting out around the building entrance? Is there any clutter, anything dangerous, any obstacles to wheelchairs or buggies, or anything that sends out an unhelpful message?

- Does the entrance look 'alive' enough to attract those who might be hoping for an excuse not to come in?

- Do you need welcomers *outside*?

- Have you designated a team who know that it is their role to make sure everyone has been welcomed? Do they welcome the youngest as well as the oldest?

- Do the rest of the team know that it's their role too and that the official welcomers are only the back-up to the welcome from the rest of the team, to make sure no one is missed?

- If there's a queue to get in, have you provided shelter on rainy days and a system for speeding up the registration process?

- Is it obvious to a newcomer where they can find coat hooks, toilets, a buggy park and a cup of tea? If not, do you need signage or a human being to tell them?

- Is anybody ever on their own for more than a few seconds?

- Are the loos fit for purpose and accessible to all ages and abilities?

THE WELCOME ZONE

The Messy Church welcome minute, ten minutes, half hour or whatever timespan works for you, is not just a time-filler but a valuable opportunity to start building relationships with our guests, demonstrating by word and action, conversation and companionable listening silence how much they are valued, loved, accepted and welcomed.

Beth Barnett from Australia has a lovely word to describe what you're starting to do in this zone: you're being an 'alongsider'—not an overbearing host, making it clear that this is *your* church, or a doorkeeper who lets people in but then leaves them alone to get on with it. An alongsider is someone who comes gently alongside a family or individual, offering themselves as a living sacrifice to make the outsider feel safe and loved, risking rejection and the embarrassment of having nothing to say. An alongsider is happy not to coerce or to manipulate but simply to join in the mutual give-and-take of conversation, relationship and friendship. Look at Jesus and the way he was happy just to sit with people. We can read about the challenges he made to them and the miracles he worked in them—the exceptional times—but there were doubtless hundreds of ordinary times when he was just eating with them, just walking with them, just chatting with them, transforming lives and enjoying *himself*. He related to people not only through dramatic signs but through unrecorded gentle, funny, intriguing, loving, sacrificial 'alongsiding'.

This is everybody's role, not just the people at the door. Linda Staal, in her cross-generational church work (see www.homegrownfaith.net), describes it as 'accompaniment' and describes the component parts of cross-generational accompaniment as vulnerability, mutuality, inclusivity, sustainability and empowerment.

- Vulnerability takes risks with people.

- Mutuality has an attitude of give and take.

- Inclusivity has eyes to notice who's missing and who is being excluded.

- Sustainability expects to build relationships that last beyond the two hours of church.

- Empowerment means rejoicing in others' achievements as well as our own.

This hospitable attitude of accompaniment is very different from the attitude of one who comes to church 'to be fed'. Hospitable people will be 'fed' and fed in abundance, but they will be fed by putting others first.

Think about the following ways of improving your welcome.

- Some of the team members are introverts and find it very hard to bounce up to strangers. Do we have things (such as jigsaws, puzzles, challenges or tasks) that will help them come alongside people?

- Are the chairs and tables set out in a way that encourages team and guests to mingle?

- Might you challenge each other to intentionally take one of Linda Staal's five aspects of accompaniment and do it at Messy Church one month, then share what happens?

WELCOMING REFRESHMENTS

In the UK, a cup of tea, or glass of water or juice on arrival is a good symbolic gesture of welcome. It represents generosity and (for the host) a hope that the guest will stay for some time; for the guest, it represents a willingness to commit to a certain length of stay rather than a speedy getaway. It also gives you something to do with your hands, whether you're a shy host or a shy guest. (Why do we usually not give people a drink as they arrive at traditional church, I wonder? Why wait till the end of the service?)

- What do your refreshments say non-verbally about your community?

- Have you got alternatives for people who have allergies or are trying to eat healthily?

- Are the cups, mugs or beakers suitable for the people coming?

- Are the biscuits 'lowest common denominator' ones?

The opening time of a Messy Church isn't just a buffer zone but an unprogrammed opportunity simply to come alongside people and imaginatively make them feel at home. The team is working as the body of Christ (as people who have been damaged and roughed up, but are being healed) to create a safe space in a hostile world for people who have been damaged and roughed up too. It's a chance to be the people Christ has made us, just as we are—disastrous and adored, broken and restored, at home and on the way there. Are we prepared to sweat blood and tears to give of our best and, at the same time, to sit back and let the Christ-light shine through us; to hang out with people in this threshold place and gently prepare hearts, bodies and minds to enjoy exploring his word?

CHAPTER 2

HOSPITALITY AT THE ACTIVITY TABLE

The families and others have come into Messy Church and been warmly and appropriately greeted. They have started to feel safe. Their suspicions that organised religion is all about 'brainwashing' are ebbing away in the face of the welcome from authentic people who seem to be genuinely pleased to see them, and the kitchen team's willingness to cope with their gluten-intolerant six-year-old without a hint that it's anything but a pleasure to provide for him. There are people of similar age and background, as well as some who are a lot older or a lot younger and normally wouldn't even smile at them in the street. Nobody is in their Sunday best (apart from the five-year-old who is resplendent in full fairy princess regalia, and a couple of Spidermen). Even the ten-year-old wearing a team badge has played his part by solemnly inquiring whether they want tea or coffee, and the ancient lady sitting next to their daughter looks happy to do jigsaw puzzles with her till the cows come home. It's time to move on from this safe space before it becomes constrictive, into a new part of the adventure—the activity time.

The transition time between the welcome and the activities is sometimes difficult. A good host is able to draw people gently but firmly away from one zone and make them eager to join in with the next one, by giving a warm welcome, providing a clear outline of the day's theme, whetting their appetite with brief descriptions of the treats in store, giving clear instructions, setting the boundaries of time and space and, more than anything, engendering a feeling of community moving on together—a sense of pilgrimage, perhaps.

If you, like us, manage the transition with a verbal announcement, you could encourage different people to make it. One of the guests might be asked to do it; it could be done by a child or teenager. This demonstrates that the hosting is a shared team role, not the job of one person alone, and implies that the team is something available to join, should a family ever want to do so. It might also reveal that unexpected people have surprising gifts of hospitality in the way they make the announcement and the mood they create at a potentially awkward moment.

In first-century Roman towns, a stranger could stand in the street and see through the front door into the hallway, or 'atrium', of a wealthy home. They might see the *pater familias*, the head of the household, seated in front of a display of his household wealth, and watch the way he treated his extended family, including those who did business with him or who wanted his patronage. Behind the atrium were the family rooms where the more intimate friends of the family might be invited to dine or stay. Messy Church operates a little like a Roman household that exists not for business but for growing the kingdom. The head of the household genuinely wants the town to be a better place. He knows that if he can draw more people into his extended family, he can work through them to improve the standard of living in the town as a whole and among the household members as individuals. He needs to give people a chance to see the way he does business, to see if this is a household they want to belong to: they need a chance to observe, to test and to weigh things up before they trust.

Messy Church is a little like the business of the atrium—open to everyone, even passers-by—and there are moments when the intimacy and family commitment glimpsed in the rooms further back is evident through what happens in the atrium. The activity hour is a time when this might well happen, when moments of intimacy and closeness are created like pop-up tents in the noisy, open, public space.

In terms of hospitality, moving into the activity hour is similar, perhaps, to coming into a carnival or festival, surrounded by family, friends and people who are disposed to be friendly even though you don't yet know them. It's like a playground, or a street of houses with the front doors standing open with exciting, colourful things to do inside each house, where people are welcome to come, stay or go as they please.

From a 'guest's' point of view, this fairground/street-party feel *might* be very attractive. Many children lead the way, dragging their adults towards the most appealing activity (or the one with the most sweets) or towards a leader they recognise. But it might also be threatening or overwhelming. The choice! The noise! The lack of direction! The excellent hosts at each table have the difficult task of welcoming each person or group individually, describing gently and non-confrontationally what is on offer there to one, while exercising charisma and enthusiasm to give someone else the courage to give the activity a go. There is no stock 'perfect leader' or 'perfect form of words'; one leader's welcome will be different from another's, and each family needs a personalised approach.

Jesus dealt with different people in very different ways—robustly challenging and teasing the Syro-Phoenician woman (Mark 7:27), but gently holding the hand of Jairus' daughter (Mark 5:41). He did this not from a worked-out strategy but because of his hospitable nature, which made him insightful, sensitive, tender, vulnerable, confident, challenging, generous and forgiving in every encounter with another human being. Even with the people who made themselves his enemies, he lived out this hospitable nature: he 'knew what [the Pharisees] were thinking' (Luke 5:22) and took the trouble to explain to them, in their own language and on their own terms, who he was. His responses always gave them face-saving wriggle-room, should they choose to accept it: 'So give back to Caesar what is Caesar's, and to God what is God's' (Matthew 22:21) and, 'What is written in the Law? How do you read it?' (Luke 10:26). He never scored points for the sake of knocking people back. Instead he graciously and honestly set out the truth in ways that could have brought the response of a laugh or smile of appreciation.

The fact that few of the elite religious teachers chose to respond generously shows the risk that is always entailed in offering hospitality. Fundamentally, though, Jesus lived out his hospitable welcome to anyone and everyone in every tiny conversation or encounter. We need to learn to do the same—to welcome a stranger into the safe space that is our very self, to treat them with respect, love, humility and gladness, and to look for and recognise the pluses that they bring to our minuses. We can do this on the grand scale of running a Messy Church and we can do it on the micro scale of a single fleeting conversation. 'In one little time, as little as it is, may heaven be won and lost,' wrote the author of *The Cloud of Unknowing* (Chapter 4). Hospitality should be in every breath we take, every word, every glance, every encounter, as well as being our overarching strategy and direction.

A leader or team member can, of course, 'frame' their activity table as they want to in their own mind. Here are some mental somersaults that we might observe as three different characters prepare the same activity.

- **Anita:** This is a task I've been given. It's my job on the rota. The minister will be pleased with me. I have to get people at my table to make a skeleton out of pasta. They mustn't eat the pasta. I'm not sure why we're making skeletons, but I expect it's something about Jesus. The main thing is to get the job done, using as little pasta as possible to save money, to get cleared up and go home on time. I'll get some ready so that all they have to do is put their name on it, and they'll have a nicer thing to take home than they would have if they'd made it themselves.

- **Bert:** My activity this month is making pasta skeletons to teach children the concept of the body of Christ. I must make sure everyone doing this activity understands which book in the Bible the verse comes from, and that they know that being part of a body means we have to work together. In fact, I'll get them to write that on their skeletons so that they remember.

- **Cathy:** I hope the family I met last time comes to give the skeleton a try. I want to find out if George won that important match he was looking forward to and whether Shona's job prospects are any better. I know they'll enjoy this activity. Pat said last time how uncomfortable she feels about playing with food when so many people in the world are hungry, so I've changed it from pasta shapes to lengths of wool. I wonder how they'll feel about being part of a body, when Grandpa is probably going to need a leg amputated because of his diabetes? They might have insights into the passage that I've never dreamed of. God, help me to have the right words and to know when to shut up.

These are crude stereotypes, of course, to make the point. Let's think about each of these table leaders in terms of their sense of hospitality.

Anita sees her activity as hers. It's all about her. 'My table' means 'my rules, my domain, my territory'. Her ownership of the task only goes as far as turning up and going through the motions. She's rather like someone whose partner has invited friends round for dinner, who vaguely resents the intrusion and goes through the motions of entertaining them, but escapes to another room as soon as possible and is heartily relieved when they've gone and the house has been put back to the way it should be. It is a job only, not something that she is doing as an expression of her character, her gifts or her love. In fact, she is doing it out of self-interest, to impress the minister. Perhaps she's been complaining about the cost of Messy Church, and coming to help puts her in the powerful position of being able to knock the system from the inside ('No one can say I haven't helped'). Any idea of service to others is far from her mind. Even the activity itself is completed for them. What really matters is leaving the church tidy ready for the Sunday service.

Bert has taken the trouble to become a good host to the extent of informing himself about the theme and bringing his imagination and creativity into play. He is being very intentional and purposeful about his activity. He has started to feel confident in his role as host and about what he wants his 'mini-household' to communicate. Where his hospitality falls down is that he has taken on all the power of a host without any of the mutuality and vulnerability of a hospitable relationship. Bert's 'customers' will be told exactly what the passage means, with no expectation of contradiction or new insight. He will teach and give, and they will learn and receive. He is intending to concentrate on the children only, so that he won't be threatened by the adults. Bert has everything to inflict on others and nothing to take from them. He risks nothing.

Cathy is creating a 'mini-household' of true hospitality. Her concerns are all based on relationships and the well-being of her 'guests'. She has even altered the activity out of loving respect for those guests' needs. She sees it not as an opportunity to make a brilliant finished product but as a meeting place, a space made for conversation to deepen those relationships. She knows she will learn from the guests. She's prepared to risk getting the details of Shona's job or George's sport wrong and looking a bit of a fool. She values the children as much as the adults, and the adults as much as the children, and she is conscious of her own need for God to be the ultimate host and provider.

Management consultant Rob Asghar describes how a good host behaves. Interestingly, this passage is written in the context of leadership in business. Look at the way Rob sees hospitality as springing not from a 'jobsworth' attitude but from the very *character* of the host:

You've willingly taken on the role of providing everyone else with the best possible experience. As the host, you realise you won't make everyone happy. You don't have the budget or time for that, and you know that you can't do much about the fact that many people were just born to complain. But you do what you set out to do, with both maturity and passion.

A good host has a certain energy, which every leader should aspire to summon as they begin their day. The good host exudes a warm, inviting spirit that signals, 'This is a good and safe place to be. You're in the right place. We've got it under control.'

An accomplished host is outward-focused, more likely to compliment you on your outfit than to worry about what you

think of his outfit. He takes spilled drinks and faux pas moments in stride. Ultimately, he takes ownership of the evening, but he does so in a way that doesn't consume or drain him.
'A GOOD HOST MAKES THE BEST LEADER' (WWW.FORBES.COM/ SITES/ROBASGHAR/2014/08/05/A-GOOD-HOST-MAKES-THE-BEST-LEADER)

Hospitality around the activity table is not something we bolt on; it stems from who we are and who we are becoming. This is why it's so important that Christians who want to make a difference in the world are always on a lifelong, intentional journey Christwards. There needs to be something going on in the 'inner rooms of the household', to use the Roman image again. When our welcome of others is part of our very character—turned inside-out and upside-down and gently developed, whittled and remoulded over the years—when our welcome is no longer about what we *do* but who we *are*, it will be a joy and an energising power bubbling up and feeding us. We won't be able to help ourselves!

If hospitality remains something we do as an add-on, out of duty or as a favour to the leader, because we have never changed in character from the grumpy, self-seeking, demanding, disapproving, pious, holier-than-thou, critical grouch that we were before we met Jesus (I speak personally, you understand)… well, then it's time to get down on our knees and hammer at the door of heaven until some hospitable angel is merciful enough to change us from the inside out. In the long term, it's far less exhausting than continuing to run activities from a well that is dried out.

In his blog 'Psephizo' (www.psephizo.com), Ian Paul summarises chapters 5 and 6 of Thom and Joani Shultz's book *Why Nobody Wants to Go to Church Anymore*. Ian lists the aspects of radical hospitality from these chapters of the book as follows:

- Seeking to understand.

- Authentically welcoming others and being glad to be with them.

- Caring curiosity.

- Being a friend even though it's not your 'job'.

- Accepting, no matter what.

- Profoundly relational.

- Something that takes time.

- Unnerving, surprising, and messy.

WWW.PSEPHIZO.COM/LIFE-MINISTRY/CAN-CHURCHES-BECOME-IRRESISTIBLE

These insights prompt the following questions, examining whether we might be even more hospitable around our activity tables (although I think we're OK on the final suggestion in the list above). Perhaps you could work through them at a team training evening over a glass of wine and a chocolate cake?

PREPARING ACTIVITIES IN A SPIRIT OF HOSPITALITY

- Are enough of your activities accessible to people with different abilities?

- Are your activities of a nature that leaves space for conversations (in other words, not so complicated that they take hours to explain at every step)?

- Do your activities encourage adults and children to work together across the generations?

- Is your furniture arranged so that everyone can reach everywhere and be safe?

- Is there provision for breastfeeding mothers?

- Is there anywhere for the elderly or ill to sit down and rest?

- If you know that people from other cultures are coming, is there anything that might offend them?

- If you know that people for whom English is a second language are coming, can you translate any written words and/or learn the word for 'hello' in their language?

- Have you prepared each activity as thoroughly as possible so that each leader is unhurried, relaxed and ready?

LEADING ACTIVITIES IN A SPIRIT OF HOSPITALITY

- Are you glad to see people coming toward your table, or are you terrified, resigned or something else?

- Is there a particular person, family or type of person that you dread working with? Can you pinpoint why? How can you flip this dread around?

- Are you ready to learn from the families who come to your table?

- Do you see the families as individuals, or as a barbarian invasion?

- Do you use people's names?

- Is your own name clearly visible and do you introduce yourself?

- Are you excited about your activity and keen to share it?

- Do you expect to have fun yourself?

- Is there any moment when Jesus would not be welcome at your table?

- Are you expecting God to be at work?

- Is your table a safe space for people's physical well-being and a place where they can share emotional or spiritual confidences safely?

- How generous are you prepared to be with the materials, with your own person, and with your church?

CHAPTER 3

HOSPITALITY AT THE LORD'S TABLE

Perhaps the most obvious symbol of hospitality is the table, which is why I've entitled chapters 1–4, about the four zones of Messy Church, 'Hospitality at [a certain sort of] table'. In Messy Church there are indeed four main uses for tables:

- The welcome tables that we sit around as we arrive and have a cup of tea.

- The activity tables (as well as floor spaces, wall spaces and occasionally balconies, church towers, gardens or sandpits) that we sit or stand around to explore the story of the day.

- The meal tables that we sit around to eat together.

- The Lord's table (the subject of this chapter) around which we hold our celebration.

(We will lay aside several more creative uses of tables, transformed to become Noah's ark, Jesus' boatful of disciples crossing the lake, the house with the flat roof into which the man on the mat was lowered, Jesus' tomb and other dramatic interpretations.)

The 'table' might be a symbolic title only. We might not actually use a table in our celebration time; the table that is part of the furniture of the church might be physically outside the circle of the Messy congregation, or way up at the other end of the choir stalls, or moved aside to make space for the projector, but it's always there symbolically. I have to admit to a personal terror about the physical presence of a beautifully dressed 'altar' with 'snow whyt linen cloth' (as the Book of Common Prayer describes it), silver candlesticks bearing lit candles, flowers beautifully and delicately arranged, and a valuable cross. Perhaps I need therapy after sitting paralysed with tension too many times, watching unrestrained toddlers tugging on the tempting folds of cloth hanging over the edge to see what will happen. Will the parent come and whisk them away in time? Should I make it look as if I care more about the furniture than the people by going and sitting underneath the table with the child? (Bad mistake, resulting in *all* the toddlers joining me in this enticing den.) But the table as a powerful concept of the gathered people of God in the presence of a holy God is always there when any group of Christians meets, whether in a home, forest, school, battlefield, church building or workplace.

The table as the focus for worship in the Judeo-Christian tradition is a long-established one. Exodus 25 sets out how the table for the tabernacle was to be made (with great care and reverence) and what it was for—to hold the loaves of bread and the frankincense that represented the proximity of God to his people, his presence among them. Solomon had gold and silver tables made for the temple (1 Chronicles 28:16; Hebrews 9:2). Ezekiel 40:38–43 describes tables around the porticos on which animals were offered as sacrifices, and Ezekiel 44:16 demonstrates the holiness or 'set apartness' of the table: '[The Levitical priests] alone are to come near my table to minister before me and serve me as guards.' Maybe the frustration that Jesus felt in the temple courts was exacerbated by his sense of the holiness of the table in that particular place: here were people exploiting and profiteering from tables (Matthew 21:12–13).

Weaving around this image of a table that holds the holy things of God, that represents his presence among his people, and also holds connotations of sacrifice, is the thread of the table of the king. This is the table of feasting and provision, of celebration and inclusion. We will think more about that in the next chapter, about meal tables, but it informs and colours the more austere 'worship' table of holiness, immanence and sacrifice and cannot be sequestered out of our celebration space.

So we set off from a paradoxical premise: a table renowned for its exclusivity (holiness, perfection, the awesome presence of God himself) also plays a part in hospitality (inclusive, egalitarian, non-judgemental). How can this table, which only a select few should approach (and they with fear and trembling), be accessible to 'all whom the Lord our God will call' (Acts 2:39)?

The simple answer is that this is God's table, not ours. He has the right to welcome whoever he likes to it. The rules, if there are rules, are his to make and break. We are reminded of the time when David and his men ate the very holy loaves of consecrated bread when they were in need, even though it should only have been the priests who ate them. Jesus praised the action and gave it as an example of the importance of meeting human need rather than blindly sticking to the rule book (Matthew 12:1–4; see 1 Samuel 21:3–6).

This incident is easy for us to cheer in Messy Church, where invitational, outward-facing hospitality is in our DNA and where we start to be very worried if we only have baptised, committed Christians attending. We delight in opening the doors to the holy things of God and holding them out to young and old, people with postgraduate degrees and those who can't read, people who could happily feature in a cereal advert as a wholesome healthy-bowelled family and those who are the despair of governmental agencies. Of course, many inherited churches also do this and would like to do it more. But because a Messy celebration doesn't centre around the Eucharist and its attendant guidelines about who can and can't take part, we can be very light on rules, playing safe, and the fear of getting it wrong; and heavy on love, risk and grace. On the rare occasions when we do celebrate the Eucharist in Messy Church, we can rediscover it as the multi-layered sacrament of community, celebration, hospitality and Christ-centredness that it is.

In *The Hospitality of God* (SPCK, 2011), Mary Gray-Reeves and Michael Perham set out to discover what emergent churches can teach inherited churches. They wrestle with the sacrament of the Eucharist, which, for Christians in some traditions, is the ceremony that throws into sharp relief the question we are grappling with here: who is welcome at the table? Who can receive Communion? Only the people who have made a commitment, have been baptised and are consciously on a journey with Jesus Christ—or anybody who happens to be in the vicinity of the table at the time and quite fancies it? The two authors study the question in the context of a community that is invitational and in which, therefore, not everybody yet believes in God. They freely admit that the situation 'needs attention' (p. 138), and they go on to say (p. 141):

It may be the will of God for the Church that the Eucharist should be the ultimate expression of communion with the Trinity and with one another within the Body of Christ, but that does not prevent it being a means of grace for those who, on their way to faith, find themselves for a moment incorporated into something that they are not yet ready to commit to or meeting with One who they are not yet ready to embrace. The outcome of that may be a church that puts more emphasis on invitation than on qualification, but is also ready, by good teaching and gentle leading, to move people, who have stumbled into Eucharistic participation without knowing its full significance, to the baptismal water and to a sense of being part of the Body.

Interestingly, Perham and Gray-Reeves offer four other insights that they believe the inherited church can receive from the emergent church:

- A commitment to team collaboration and participation in the preparation of the liturgy.

- An emphasis on the importance of 'open space' or 'stations' to explore the message and to respond, rather than having one person preaching or interceding.

- A return to liturgical complexity and richness.

- The development of a 'Rule', such as the new monastics use.

How might we express the principles of hospitality in our gathered celebration time? In my book *Messy Celebration* (Messy Church, 2013), I've explored in detail different ways to make people who aren't used to organised worship feel at home in this 15-minute zone of Messy Church. I don't propose to repeat them here, but that book would make a good source of practical ideas as you discuss the questions at the end of this chapter.

Here are five aspects of hospitality that we might usefully consider for the celebration time.

First, being a great host entails making strangers feel they belong in the community. It might be helpful to picture the transition time from activities to celebration as being like the hospitable call of Jesus to the confused, beleaguered, tired, hungry, messy, scruffy crowds around him when he said, 'Come to me, all you who are weary and burdened, and I will give you rest. Take my yoke upon you and learn from me, for I am gentle and humble in heart, and you will find rest for your souls. For my yoke is easy and my burden is light' (Matthew 11:28–30). The celebration is like a moment of sabbath rest for people's souls in the busyness and hard work of Messy Church. It is informed by the hard work that everyone has been doing in the activity time (the equivalent of the six working days of the week) but is a moment of true rest, true celebration, of learning in relationship with Jesus himself and with his people. It's not an endurance test but a time to relax, relish and enjoy, treating each other with gentleness and humility, as does our host himself.

Second, a good host provides food (for the soul). Jesus said, 'I am the bread of life. Whoever comes to me will never go hungry, and whoever believes in me will never be thirsty' (John 6:35). A good host puts the best food he has on the table, and doesn't keep the crunchiest poppadums and the creamiest puddings just for close family to enjoy afterwards. The best food we have to offer at this point in a Messy Church is (as Jesus explains at length in John 6) Jesus himself. For some churches, that might mean a determination to offer the Eucharist regularly to Messy Church families. For others, it might mean a determination to enable 'encounter' with Christ to happen rather than just talking about him. (I discovered that it was much safer and easier to read books about prayer than to actually pray.) For yet others, it might mean permission to focus celebrations less on entertainment and more on worship. However we interpret the 'best food' in the light of our church tradition, we can enjoy knowing that people don't live on bread alone and that in Messy Church we can offer the sort of bread that will enable us all to 'live for ever' (John 6:58).

Third, a good host is transformed by his guests. Here is an imaginative (perhaps overfanciful) interpretation of that strange and troubling account of Jesus' behaviour towards a vulnerable member of society, the Syro-Phoenician woman in Matthew 15.

Jesus has just had a no-holds-barred showdown with the Pharisees, those great guardians of rules about purity and holiness. They came from Jerusalem, like malevolent inspectors with clipboards, and seemed determined not to find the truth but to find fault. They challenged Jesus about the way they'd seen his disciples eating: 'Why do your disciples break the tradition of the elders? They don't wash their hands before they eat!' (Matthew 15:2). Jesus was frustrated by their inability to see what was so obvious to him, and tried to help them see the bigger picture: 'And why do you break the command of God for the sake of your tradition?' (v. 3). (The equivalent passage in Mark 7:8 says, 'You have let go of the commands of God and are holding on to human traditions.') Don't you love the comment from the disciples in Matthew 15:9, pointing out the obvious: 'Do you know that the Pharisees were offended when they heard this?' I'll bet they were! But if they had really been seeking the truth, they wouldn't have been anything other than amazed.

Shortly after this showdown over food rules, Jesus escapes to hide out at a safe house, wanting to be alone. As usual, though, nobody can keep his whereabouts a secret and, before he can even put his slippers on, there's a knock at the door.

Leaving that place, Jesus withdrew to the region of Tyre and Sidon. A Canaanite woman from that vicinity came to him, crying out, 'Lord, Son of David, have mercy on me! My daughter is demon-possessed and suffering terribly.'

Jesus did not answer a word. So his disciples came to him and urged him, 'Send her away, for she keeps crying out after us.'

He answered, 'I was sent only to the lost sheep of Israel.'

The woman came and knelt before him. 'Lord, help me!' she said.

He replied, 'It is not right to take the children's bread and toss it to the dogs.'

'Yes it is, Lord,' she said. 'Even the dogs eat the crumbs that fall from their master's table.'

Then Jesus said to her, 'Woman, you have great faith! Your request is granted.' And her daughter was healed at that moment.
MATTHEW 15:21–28

Here is another table that shows us Jesus as the omnipotent host in a mutual, give-and-take relationship with a complete outsider, someone who knows absolutely that she is the last person who deserves to eat with Jesus, according to the culture. A woman! A foreigner! A non-Jew! And presumably, we might extrapolate, someone who is probably seen as a 'bad mother' if she has a demon-possessed daughter. This person has absolutely no guest rights. She feels she has the same status as a scavenging dog *under* the table.

But Jesus is fed up with the 'wisdom' of the religious people and is determined to look for wisdom in a riskier place. He can see the strength in this outsider and he knows (or hopes) he can push her until she makes those Pharisees and his own blind disciples see! He knows that she will flip the situation into a living parable that throws the hypocritical nitpicking of the Pharisees from Jerusalem and the selfish heartlessness of his own disciples into sharp relief.

He gives space for everyone in the situation to reveal their true colours: he remains silent. Then he challenges both the disciples and the woman, waiting for *someone* to see past the rules and boundaries that try to set limits on his work: 'I was sent only to the lost sheep of Israel' (v. 24). He is silently begging for someone to cut through the human limitations and reveal the heart of God. Surely the disciples (those men! those Jews! those committed followers of Jesus!) will demonstrate an understanding of God's compassion to all people? But all they do is put up more barriers for their own convenience, trying to protect themselves and Jesus, just as they do when people bring little children to be blessed. 'Send her away!'

Like a gracious host, Jesus himself gives the woman space. She in turn gives him the living example of faith and understanding of God's compassion that he needs his own disciples to hear and see. The shock of hearing *her* rather than Jesus saying these words still resonates down the millennia: she becomes the teacher. Jesus the host encourages someone who isn't even so much as a guest to provide for the community of disciples.

At our celebrations, we should make space for everyone to contribute, not just the religious experts.

Fourth, a good host is conscious of her own status as a guest around God's table. One of the biggest barriers to a feeling of being welcome in church is the sense that it's a space that 'belongs' to someone else, not to the outsider. We need to avoid the temptation to be such hospitable hosts that we forget our own status as guests. If we could remember how little we deserve to be at God's table, how much it cost him to make it possible for us to be there, how the very clothes we're wearing are those that he's provided, perhaps we might approach the celebration in a humble frame of mind. This is not our church; it is God's church. So, rather than a polished performance by the king's professional household minstrels, a celebration is a banquet to which we have *all* been invited from the 'street corners' (Matthew 22:9). The 17th-century poet George Herbert expresses it better than I can in his poem 'Love III':

Love bade me welcome; yet my soul drew back,
    Guilty of dust and sin.
But quick-eyed Love, observing me grow slack
    From my first entrance in,
Drew nearer to me, sweetly questioning
    If I lack'd anything.

'A guest,' I answered, 'worthy to be here:'
    Love said, 'You shall be he.'
'I, the unkind, ungrateful? Ah, my dear,
    I cannot look on thee.'
Love took my hand, and smiling did reply,
    'Who made the eyes but I?'

73

'Truth, Lord; but I have marred them; let my shame
Go where it doth deserve.'
'And know you not,' says Love, 'who bore the blame?'
'My dear, then I will serve.'
'You must sit down,' says Love, 'and taste my meat.'
So I did sit and eat.

Fifth, a good host sends her guests out with food for the journey. I still remember visiting the new parish-to-be en route to a holiday in France. The churchwarden's wife not only gave us a meal but pressed cartons of orange juice and treats into our hands for the ferry crossing we were heading towards. Her hospitality extended beyond her own house. On the road to Emmaus (Luke 24:13–35), Jesus walked with the disciples, taught them (in what was, no doubt, a lively give-and-take conversation) and went into the house to eat with them. That meal (where he was invited in as a guest, but also broke the bread as a host) had the effect of sending the disciples galloping back to Jerusalem, revived, refreshed, full of good news that they couldn't bear to keep to themselves. A good hospitable celebration doesn't just welcome people in but sends them out rejoicing, revived, refreshed and bubbling over with good news to share with the world around them.

In March 2015, Martyn Payne wrote in a BRF Messy Church team reflection:

Messy Church is reminding us that Christian nurture in the faith is not primarily about the liturgy or the lectionary, nor about the sacrament or the sermon, nor even solely about personal Bible reading and private prayer, but rather about being and becoming Christians together: *putting the communion back into the Eucharist; the conversation back into our worship; the community back into our conversion; the serving back into our services; and putting the shared experience of our friendship with Jesus and each other into true discipleship.*

In other words, our gathered worship becomes an expression of true hospitality.

DISCUSSION QUESTIONS

- 'The celebration is like a moment of sabbath rest for people's souls.' How can we be less driven and more relaxed in our celebrations, to make space for contributions from our guests?

- 'The best food we have to offer at this point in a Messy Church is (as Jesus explains at length in John 6) Jesus himself.' How can we offer Jesus to our families in the celebration?

- 'At our celebrations, we should make space for everyone to contribute, not just the religious experts.' In what practical ways can you make space for contributions from the least likely members of your Messy household during the celebration?

- 'Rather than a polished performance by the king's professional household minstrels, a celebration is a banquet to which we have *all* been invited from the "street corners" (Matthew 22:9).' Do we run the risk of appearing arrogant? How might we better express humility in our celebration?

- 'A good hospitable celebration doesn't just welcome people in but sends them out rejoicing, revived, refreshed and bubbling over with good news to share with the world around them.' What can we do in our celebrations to help people go out bubbling?

CHAPTER 4

HOSPITALITY AT THE MEAL TABLE

You prepare a table before me
in the presence of my enemies.
You anoint my head with oil; my cup overflows.
Surely your goodness and love will follow me
all the days of my life,
and I will dwell in the house of the Lord for ever.

PSALM 23:5–6

Perhaps the moment when the hospitality of a Messy Church is most vividly exposed in its true colours is the moment when everyone fizzes out of the celebration—that time of gathering, of being guests in the house of a greater host, but also hosts to each other and, peculiarly, to the Host himself. The congregation has brushed against something of the mysterious 'other', taking them beyond the walls of the building—like being given a glimpse of an open gate with a tantalising and intriguing path leading away from them. They have been given a sense that they matter, that they are significant both as families and as individuals and have a part to play in a story far bigger than they had thought. They have discovered, in fact, that they have the resources and ability to be not passive consumers but valued guests and welcoming hosts to others. Now, this extended family chatters its way through to the hall, where (miraculously!) the tables have been laid and the delicious smell of food is wafting out to meet them.

I was privileged to sit and eat (jacket potatoes, cheese and baked beans) with a new family at a recent Messy Church, the second one we've run in the new church I've joined. It was quite a quiet Messy Church, with only about 40 of us altogether, so I had already enjoyed meeting this family over my activity (painting slices of bread with food colouring for 'People don't live by bread alone'). They were a mum, dad and two children of about 8 and 6. I don't remember what we talked about; I just know that they opened up a glimpse of their family life to me and I shared a bit of mine. I got to enjoy the company and challenging observations of children way younger than my own and to take the first steps of friendship with the parents. Nothing dramatic, nothing supernatural, but the meal provided the space, time and framework of generosity that made it possible for my life to touch the lives of others and for theirs to touch mine. I look forward to meeting them again. I might even remember their names.

I love to remind people of the hodge-podge way we planned our first Messy Church all those years ago, and of God's intervention. We had planned the activities and the celebration, then pictured saying goodbye to everyone, clearing up and going home to cook a meal for our own families in a state of comatose exhaustion. 'Ha!' said someone. 'What if we ate together actually *at* the Messy Church? Then someone else would do the shopping, the cooking and the washing-up, and all we'd have to do would be clear up, go home and put our children to bed.' And thus, out of an acute and embarrassing laziness, did the meal in Messy Church come to pass. But God was good! Out of that shameful idleness has come this deeply symbolic ritual, steeped in the hospitality of our ancestors in the faith and in the glorious promise of the kingdom banquet that we have to look forward to (as well as being a jolly good thing in the present).

Just as a meal table set up in the middle of an open field would be rather puzzling, the meal in Messy Church gains its significance from its context within a setting of learning and worship. Similarly, the learning and worship gain hugely in significance by their proximity to the meal. The meal gives the church the 'right' to create a learning and worshipping environment, and the learning and worshipping environment gives the meal its raison d'être. The meal is an expression of community, of gratuity (or generosity) and of valuing guests just as they are. It is an expression of a desire for relationship. The church is effectively saying, 'We want to spend time with you. We want to share what we have with you. You are worth our love and attention. You are precious and valued in the eyes of God and his people. Stay with us.'

The meal table at Messy Church is doing far more than just filling hungry tummies. If we think of the faith of God's people as a light being carried from age to age, this part of the liturgy of any Messy Church carries the torch of the historic traditions of ancient faith communities. It is a blazing beacon of sacramental delight and privilege in the present and a happy first glimpse of the light at the end of the tunnel—the coming and still-to-come kingdom. A meal is the ultimate mark of hospitality.

Jesus ate with people and, as Michael Frost writes in *Exiles: Living missionally in a post-Christian culture*, 'models for us the profound power of sharing a table with the marginalised and despised' (p. 49). He goes on to summarise the 'third place' factors, originally listed by sociologist Ray Oldenburg, that help build *communitas* (meaning 'community with a higher purpose') in a location that is neither home nor workplace. The characteristics of this place include:

- being free or inexpensive.
- providing food and drink.
- being accessible, so that a visit there is easy to make part of a routine (most people should be able to walk there).
- being a place where lots of people go regularly on a daily basis.
- enabling people to feel welcome and comfortable, so that it's easy to enter into a conversation there.
- being somewhere we can expect to find old and new friends.

The meal table at Messy Church should be like the open meals that Jesus joined in. They can easily be the epitome of this 'third place', which is open, yet intimate; away from home, but a place where people feel at home. In short, Frost is aware of 'the ferocious power of hospitality' (*Exiles*, p. 171).

When human beings eat together as a group, they are expressing something about a strong cultural identity. They are effectively saying, 'We belong together.' The anthropologist James J. Fox expresses it thus: 'Commensal behaviour, as it is well-acknowledged in the anthropological literature, symbolically expresses a solidarity, commonality (or, indeed, communality) and shared identity of those who participate in it' ('Eating: The consumption of food as practical symbol and symbolic practice': see Bibliography on page 192).

It is no coincidence that Jesus left his followers with a meal by which to remember him, based in turn on a meal that had given the Jewish people a strong sense of identity over generations. A meal is a ritual that everyone, young and old, can join in. A 'festival meal' builds up a resonance of memories and shared experiences over generations, which links a community together.

Think of the experience of the people of God in Nehemiah 8:5–12:

Ezra opened the book. All the people could see him because he was standing above them; and as he opened it, the people all stood up. Ezra praised the Lord, the great God; and all the people lifted their hands and responded, 'Amen! Amen!' Then they bowed down and worshipped the Lord with their faces to the ground.

The Levites... instructed the people in the Law while the people were standing there...

Then Nehemiah the governor, Ezra the priest and teacher of the Law, and the Levites who were instructing the people said to them all, 'This day is holy to the Lord your God. Do not mourn or weep.' For all the people had been weeping as they listened to the words of the Law.

Nehemiah said, 'Go and enjoy choice food and sweet drinks, and send some to those who have nothing prepared. This day is holy to our Lord. Do not grieve, for the joy of the Lord is your strength.'

The Levites calmed all the people, saying, 'Be still, for this is a holy day. Do not grieve.'

Then all the people went away to eat and drink, to send portions of food and to celebrate with great joy, because they now understood the words that had been made known to them.

The whole people of God were gathered, young and old together, and shared in this emotional experience of first grief, then joy, culminating in a meal that was totally inclusive, even for the people who weren't prepared or able to have food ready. Like a street party for a royal Jubilee that creates lifelong memories about 'belonging' in, say, Lime Street or Johnson's Close or Wragby Road, a shared meal is part of being human beings in society. It draws a community together, proclaims equality, inclusion and justice and brings great joy to all who are included.

Kenneth E. Bailey writes brilliantly on the subject of Psalm 23 in his book *The Good Shepherd* (IVP Academic, 2014). On verses 5–6, quoted at the start of this chapter, he shares the insight that, in traditional Middle Eastern culture, great wealth is demonstrated not by buying possessions (an individualistic act) but by inviting guests to a meal where there is far more than they can eat—'community life that is strengthened and solidified by shared meals' (p. 55). (I'm reminded of the Queen of Sheba's 'overwhelmed' reaction to King Solomon's table in 1 Kings 10:5.) Kenneth Bailey points out that when the psalmist writes, 'You prepare a table before me', he is showing God rather shockingly doing a *woman's* work in preparing food for the table. ('Hurrah!' say I.) He acknowledges the great cost of this meal to the host, and the superabundant hospitality demonstrated in 'anointing my head' (a custom of hospitality shown to honoured guests) and pouring so much wine that 'my cup overflows'.

Although Bailey doesn't say so, it seems obvious that this meal must have been a glorious mess, where every inch of the table surface is covered with steaming aromatic dishes, perfumed oil is dripping down the guests' necks and wine is sloshing all over the place. It makes Messy meal times look positively restrained and orderly. (And as for most Communion services…)

Bailey also explores in depth the phrase 'in the presence of my enemies', but, while there was great significance here for David and, many years later, for Jesus among the Pharisees, I'm not sure that Messy Churches could be said to be being lavishly 'spoiled' in the face of their enemies. Who would the enemy be? We might say, I suppose, that the daily grind of poverty, hunger, abuse, individualism, materialism and violence are the enemies, and church is one of the few gatherings that can lift us away from those daily battles and give us relief, respite and refreshment. That interpretation would give us fresh impetus to make any expression of church a sanctuary space, a spa of overflowing hospitality to challenge the values and habits by which some people have been taught to live, or about which they have hitherto had no choice.

What we see—or, rather, *who* we see—in these verses from Psalm 23 is God as the perfect and rather breathtaking host who exceeds the conventions of hospitality by providing, preparing and serving a costly meal as if his whole delight is to have us at his table. He is the gender norm-busting host of ancient Middle Eastern culture. He is the king whose table meant relationship, provision and restoration. The king welcomed people to his table as a sign of confident, committed, long-term friendship. When David took the throne, he sought out Mephibosheth from Jonathan's household, to provide for him and to show his loyalty to Jonathan's line (2 Samuel 9:7). His provision for the needy, lame Mephibosheth came out of relationship, not from a 'free for all' or impersonal state provision. For Jehoiachin, eating at the king's table meant restoration to dignity after imprisonment (2 Kings 25:29).

So, for our meal table in Messy Church, we are in a noble tradition of demonstrating an invitation to enter a long-term committed relationship with the people who come to Messy Church. We want to provide in some way for those who are physically hungry and need food, but also for those who are isolated and hungry for company. We try to restore broken people to a place of dignity through giving them a place at the table. If the table in the temple is a place of holiness and sacrifice, the king's table is a place of relationship, abundant provision and restoration—a place of healing, *shalom* on four legs. At the one and at the other we can say, 'Heaven will be like this.'

Here are a few pertinent stories from meal times at Messy Churches that our colleague Martyn Payne has visited. You may find it useful, as a team, to discuss the questions they raise.

Children were seated first, as if attending a children's party, and even sat on separate tables from the grown-ups. I decided to challenge this and sat with the children—and it encouraged others to follow. Talking with the cook afterwards, she said that they never intended it to be like that but somehow the adults in the team have hung back and therefore the adult visitors follow their lead.

- How does your team model meal-time behaviour for other adults to follow?
- How does your meal time encourage friendships across the generations—or hinder them?

The leaders are from Sunday church and are organised and gifted, and they couldn't quite get their heads round why some of the families did not stay together or want to sit together for the meal. It's a situation I have come across before and it is one that Messy Churches in more challenging communities often cite as an issue to address. Sitting down to a meal is increasingly a strange activity for many today, but, at the same time, it is a very human activity that is so important for friendship-making, as well as being a mark of hospitality. Some social groups, however, do find it hard to receive in this way and would rather be busy doing than sat down receiving. It's a challenge to be able to accommodate different attitudes while still creating a safe space for everyone to feel they can be welcomed. It was a source of some tension among the leaders I spoke to, who did not understand the fears and feelings of those who did not want to be sitting at table in a passive role, waiting to be served.

- How much do you think sitting at a meal table is a 'middle-class' construct?
- What practical things might a team do to make it easier for the adults to sit and eat?

At a large (100+) Messy Church:

Feeding such a large number of people is a huge challenge. I think the kitchen team did an amazing job. It did mean, however, that there were lots of queues and a lot of people on the move in the hall. Might it be possible, I wonder, to have some different serving points around the edge of the hall to allow more people to get food more quickly and fewer people to be standing up and moving around at the same time? The meal is a really important part of Messy Church—sadly, I have visited some which have skimped on it. It is as much part of the worship as any other section and provides opportunities for great conversations, as indeed I had at my table.

- Are people at your meal time being served as efficiently as possible?

- What 'great conversations' have you had at your Messy meal?

The meal was back in the church hall—lots of interesting sandwiches and cakes and drink—ideal for [hot] weather, although it is always a cold buffet like this, apparently. On my table, I spoke with a couple who come from a town many miles away to visit Mum nearby, and they always make it link in with Messy Church. A dad was there with his two children, and he is a regular visitor and loves it. They sometimes go to a local church nearer to them, but there's not much there for families. Other families were full of praise for this Messy Church: 'There's always something new happening,' they said, 'with interesting crafts and stories every time, and something for everyone.' It didn't take long for them to start talking about other Messy Churches over the last 18 months, including a very successful one in Lent, where they all made pancakes and tossed them during the celebration.

- What help might members of your team need if they are to chat with strangers as easily as Martyn does?
- How do you feel about a cold buffet for a meal?

I think the meal took some of them by surprise—but it was really welcome. The minister commented that she knew that some families there would really appreciate a hot meal being provided. I sat with a Muslim family who were really happy to be there and were making friends with those of another faith. I also talked a lot to young Ellie, who seemed to be on her own until I spotted her nan lurking at the door, not wanting to get too involved. Here was someone on the edge, who I've no doubt, with time, will be drawn in. Ellie wasn't sure she'd like the pasta but ended up having second helpings.

- How do/would you express hospitality to people from other faiths and cultures at the meal time?

- How do/would you feel about eating with people from other faiths?

At a bi-monthly gathering:

Their chosen Messy Church pattern is to begin with some food, although this is just cakes, biscuits and drink, not a hot meal. The activities take place in the church hall, which is connected and behind the main building, and they end with the celebration together.

- What might this team gain and lose from approaching the meal as they do?

At almost every activity table I went to, the story was being talked about, even in a rush, and at the meal tables there were questions that got us talking. On our table it was the children who asked the questions, which led to conversations about prayer and whether we had ever experienced answers to prayer. Oh, and there were also some great 'knock knock' jokes, which were perfect for the parable we'd been talking about!

- How do you feel about having 'questions' at the meal tables to promote conversation on the day's theme?

Because of a leaking roof in the chancel, they can't hold their celebration there at the moment. So instead we were all rather squashed up between the tables in one corner of the tiny church, which meant that it was a struggle to maintain a focus and a sense of everyone being part of the story and prayers. The same space then became our eating area almost immediately afterwards.

- What can you praise God for about your facilities?
- Dream dreams: what would be the ideal facilities in which to demonstrate hospitality without inhibitions? Are they out of the question?

CHAPTER 5

HOSPITALITY IN A MESSY HOME

Archbishop Justin Welby spoke challengingly to an all-party parliamentary group at Church House in his talk 'On a Good Economy' in February 2015. He spoke of the different traits of a 'good economy', including creativity, gratuity, solidarity and subsidiarity. The last one, 'subsidiarity' (the principle that a central authority should perform only those tasks that cannot be performed at a local level), is interesting in the context of hospitality at church and at home. The Archbishop writes:

An economy based on the principle of subsidiarity is therefore one in which there is a strong awareness of who does what best and collaborative working between different elements of the economy to enable the flourishing of all. It is seen in anti-monopoly legislation, in local government, in decentralisation, and in regulation that ensures accountability of huge companies to customers. It is seen also in the state not being in places which enable individuals, groups and communities to do what they are best called to do.

In other words, there are things that the state can and should do to help build a good economy, but people also need to be encouraged to do the personal stuff alongside the impersonal state policy and practice. We can and do think usefully about the way our local church can be hospitable on a slightly more institutional level, but we also need to be hospitable on a personal level for the best functioning of our 'economy of kingdom'. If the core values of Messy Church are worth anything, they will work their way out from the gathered church into the homes and lives of the people who belong to it, making them more creative, celebratory, aware of the different generations, Christ-centred and, yes, hospitable.

As we become more hospitable in our homes, the hospitality of the church will flow even more naturally in a virtuous circle that blesses all who come under its influence.

This chapter takes a brief look at the challenge to make not just our churches but also our homes into more welcoming places, expressive of hospitality.

It all starts with a sense of who our home belongs to: is it our own possession, which we have bought and paid for, so that it belongs to us, or is it a gift from God to be used to bless our own family and others? Our culture encourages us to keep ourselves to ourselves; dinner parties are for the chattering classes or people on TV, but not for us; inviting someone round for a meal can be hugely threatening to them and might even mean they steer clear of us to avoid embarrassment in future. In this culture, where 'hospitality' is inextricably linked to 'industry' or 'business', how do we show the open-handed love of God that we've been exploring in a church setting?

There are some awesome role models to learn from.

In her book *Don't Invite Them to Church: Moving from a come and see to a go and be church* (Faith Alive, 2010), Karen Wilk writes of the need to bless our neighbours by doing them good and helping the kingdom to come where we live, rather than inviting them to come to our church. This calling took her and her family on the adventure of opening up their home to their neighbours. She writes of starting to build relationships through offering hospitality for occasional events, which led to regular meetings with her neighbours for tea and discussion, and sharing dog-walking responsibilities. She challenges the reader to be less busy with church activities and to have more time for connecting with people in the neighbourhood, serving them in practical ways, eating with them, praying for them and creating *communitas*—a community with a higher purpose.

Another example of living out hospitality radically as part of an intentional way of life is the Duckworth family from New Zealand. In the book *Against the Tide, Towards the Kingdom* (Cascade, 2011), Jenny Duckworth describes hospitality as far more than an add-on ministry in their extended household missional community. From the start of their married life together, including their time as parents, she and her husband Justin have lived among the marginalised and invited needy people to live in their household and do family life together.

We decided to explore a socially simple life, choosing to create community around our households. This meant the people we lived with were also the people we did ministry with, socialised with, and worshipped with… We had to eat; now we ate with our young people and friends. We had to go shopping and do housework, more opportunity to communicate, hang out or at least save each other time. Setting up a community household wasn't always easy. (p. 35)

Jenny describes how their children were a vital part of the hospitality of the household:

I am convinced that our community life has been a precious gift to them and that they in turn have offered so much to our neighbourhoods. We have young people who will say to us now that they would never have stayed with us through the rough times without our kids. It seems that little ones can express unconditional love in a way that is much easier to understand. (p. 38)

She finishes the chapter on hospitality with a challenge:

In the end we can have a castle mentality about our homes, where we draw up the drawbridge and close out the wicked world. Or we can treat our houses as motels, which we check in and out of in between living a life out there. Or we can create a home that is a warm and safe offering we extend to others. Offering home in our modern world is one of the most radical things we can do. Not just Sunday lunch, but a place for others to share life with, which nurtures the reality of God's welcoming family. That's the heart of the gospel. (p. 39)

Let me put my cards on the table here: I am rubbish at hospitality. No, really, I am. At a life-changing level, I would love to give a child a home by adoption, but don't see how I could be a half-adequate parent without giving up my job (to which I feel called). At a lower level, I would love to have people round for meals, but the time involved in shopping, cooking, cleaning, welcoming, eating together and clearing up is more than I have available while I'm working in this weird job. Frankly, this is no excuse but it is still the reason. I know in my head that a clean house doesn't matter and that it's better to get in a takeaway and actually have people round than to worry about cooking 'properly' and therefore not have them round at all: I just need to convince my heart about that. The same goes for having the next-door neighbour round for a cup of tea: I'm supposed to be working at home during the day, not idling around, knee-deep in Oreos and Hobnobs. Spontaneous visitors: hurrah, yes please! Come and take us as we are, and you can make do with the manky digestives left in the biscuit tin or we'll pad the stew out with lentils, boil a few more potatoes and delight in the fact that you felt you could turn up unexpectedly. But if we properly invite someone round, I want to show how much we treasure them by taking the trouble to cook something nice, not just slinging a bag of chips on the table and lashing out the ketchup.

My granny used to cook no fewer than seven puddings for every meal with guests. It's in my genes: my very DNA shouts that one pudding is inadequate. But day to day, we don't have pudding at all. Don't get me wrong: it's not about impressing our guests. That's not a competition that interests me in the slightest, and it would never have occurred to Granny, who simply wanted to spoil her guests in the best way she knew how. For me, having people round for a meal is about expressing love and care and respect, by showing that they're worth cooking for. I read books like the two cited above and feel dark despair that not only are these women living the life and practising what they preach about hospitality: *they've even managed to find time to write books about it.* (So I can't even use writing this book as an excuse!)

On the plus side, as a household, we have enjoyed providing a home for an asylum seeker from the Democratic Republic of Congo for several months and a temporary home for several friends in need of a bed; we joyfully welcome Messy Church visitors from overseas to our home to make their trip cheaper and more fun and to give us more time to talk. Our Messy planning meetings here each month feature a bottle of wine more often than not, and we have had a couple of 'open house' days for the neighbours since we moved here, involving vast amounts of cake. But this is hardly the sort of radical hospitality that creates intimacy and develops relationships that strengthen the kingdom and threaten the very gates of hell.

So this chapter about hospitality in homes is written from a deep sense of humility. Although people like Jenny Duckworth and Karen Wilk have turned hospitality into the very lifeblood of the way they work as families, I haven't. While I know in my brain that hospitality unlocks blessings in both directions, I can't quite see how to do it yet.

I suspect that several things might be key to getting started with hospitable homes if you, like me, feel that the spirit is willing but the flesh is weak. (To people much further down the road of radical hospitality, who are not just having people round for a meal, but are daily extending invitations to join their household to live there, adopting and fostering needy children, or living in missional communities, these suggestions are going to sound pretty feeble!)

- **Prayer:** Hospitality is something like vegetarianism. I am convinced that it is a good thing, but in practice my habits lag a long way behind my convictions. (Oh bacon butties, you tempt me.) I need turning inside out so that God makes me *want* to do more to open up the home we've been blessed with, so that it becomes a joy and something to look forward to, rather than an ordeal or a religious duty inflicted by extraverts on introverts. The only way I am going to be transformed in that way is through prayer.

- **Practice:** I will not have the entire destitute population of Hampshire living in our spare room by the end of the week. I will not spend every evening cooking for and with different church members. I need to start with smaller steps into hospitality and check where our household tipping point is—that moment when it all becomes too much and puts the family under unbearable strain. Starting small makes sense, with invitations to 'safe' people, with whom I can develop a set of tasty but easy recipes that I feel confident to produce. I need to 'practise' hospitality, in the sense of getting better at it bit by bit, like someone practising the piano.

- **Pattern:** We need to make a resolution as a household to practise hospitality regularly, deciding together how often to do it, so that everybody has a stake in it. Then we need to build our resolution into family routine so that it becomes a character-forming habit, like a Rule of Life. One person I read about resolved to have someone round for a meal every week and to put on a bigger neighbourhood 'event' every month. (I feel my heart sinking as I imagine our neighbours desperately trying to find excuses to refuse yet another invitation…) For my family, in our context, and for the sanity of our very British neighbours, we would need to set ourselves a more attainable target.

- **Helpful examples:** We tend to operate better as community than solo acts. Can I find someone in my Messy Church team to share this vision with, who will come on board and try to be hospitable too? That way, they will challenge me to stick to my resolutions and share my questions, joys and failures.

Alongside my own personal resolve, we can try to do better as a team, to talk honestly about what makes us feel that hospitality is difficult, maybe too difficult.

In our Messy Churches, too, we can keep encouraging an attitude of hospitality, by looking out for those God-moments when someone not on the team invites us round for a coffee. We can decide to see the invitation not as a bit of a bind or a time-consuming duty, but as a miracle to respond to eagerly. We can have hospitable eyes in our heads, on the look-out for appropriate opportunities to invite somebody else round for a coffee or lunch. Perhaps someone mentions being lonely during the day, or that their husband or wife works away from home during the week, or that the new baby makes cooking difficult, or simply that times are hard at the moment. These are opportunities to stick a toe in the water of invitation. We can also include suggestions for being hospitable on handouts or take-home sheets when the Messy Church theme links in with eating or homes or welcome.

Sometimes hospitality can be unleashed by a one-off catalytic event, like a 'safari meal' for your Messy Church—a travelling party that eats nibbles or starters in one home, the main course in another, dessert in another and coffee and mints in another, with the whole group walking or driving together between houses. It's an opportunity to invite Messy families to be hosts as well as guests for one of the courses, not just to assume that the team members will provide the venues and food.

Letting our homes become outposts of our Messy Church, to reflect the hospitable values that we practise there once a month, could only have a vast and beneficial effect on our ministry, our witness, our neighbourhood and our own discipleship.

QUESTIONS

- Who do you know who is truly hospitable?

- On a scale of 0–10, how hospitable are you?

- What puts you off being more hospitable in your home?

- Is there anything you can do to encourage each other as a team?

- Which of the four practical ways forward, listed above, do you feel is doable?

- What other ideas do you have?

CHAPTER 6

HOSPITALITY TO GROW YOUR TEAM

One of the main preoccupations of a Messy Church leader is how to get, keep and grow a team to run the Messy Church. But what if we look at this through the lens of hospitality? Might that alter the way we think of the task of team-building? Might it shed light on constructive ways to do it and even help us to rephrase our aims? After all, as we've been exploring so far in this book, the language of 'getting' and 'keeping' doesn't really tally with a hospitable mindset. A hospitable person is more likely to say something like, 'Here is a space and opportunity for God's team to start. How do I invite and welcome people to his team? How do I make them feel at home, safe enough to offer their true gifts in his service? How do we create together a group with a strong identity and purpose, which always remains hospitable to new ideas and people? How can we all continually become better hosts and better guests to Christ, to the families we're serving and to each other? How will we reflect the glorious hospitality of God in Christ Jesus, which has brought us to this point in our walk with him and draws us even closer to him?'

It's not about team building; it's about an attitude of hospitality reverberating through and shaping the mini-household that is our team. The paraphrase of Philippians 2 that I quoted from in Chapter 1 starts like this before it gets to the famous hymn:

Work together on your team. Don't expect this team stuff to happen easily. If Jesus means anything to you, then what should be your priority? To love each other, to stick together when you disagree, to remind each other every time what you're in it for, who you're in it for. Yes, use your own gifts and have fun in this mission but make sure everyone on the team is having as much fun as you by being the person they were made to be and using their gifts too. If you can't work out how, go back to Jesus as the shining example who let go of everything… (Philippians 2:1–5)

In the next chapter you'll find a session to run for and with your Messy Church team, helpers, extras and interested fringe people, as a special treat for them and to help you all think about becoming more hospitable. You could even use it as a session for the rest of your church, if you're thinking about how to be more welcoming in all your services and ministries.

Here are some aspects of hospitality that are worth pondering. They could help you to take hospitality seriously in the way you run your planning, preparation and personnel for Messy Church.

- Keep reminding yourselves of your household identity.

- Be good hosts: be generous.

- Be good guests: be willing to receive.

- Make others feel that the space is their 'home'.

- Be relational alongside being functional.

- Know each other and each other's gifts, strengths and weaknesses.

- Face outwards towards new possibilities and people.

- Put others in the team before yourself, confident that they will put you before themselves.

- Expect to meet Christ in the others.

- Pitch tents; don't build skyscrapers.

- Commit to the long haul.

- Enjoy it; if you don't, find ways to enjoy it.

- Expect it to be messy: relax into it, embrace it, enjoy it.

- Add your own insights.

Keep reminding yourselves of your household identity. 'The practice of hospitality challenges the boundaries of a community while it simultaneously depends on that community's identity to make a space that nourishes life' (Christine Pohl, *Making Room*, p. 130).

If we want to have messy edges that create a welcoming and threshold space for all, we need to have a very strong core identity at the heart. The team needs to know who they are, what they're doing, how they're doing it and why they're doing it. The clearer the identity at the heart of a Messy Church, the riskier, more open and more hospitable it can be in all its aspects. When a parent starts to change a child's nappy in The Wrong Place, a team member who is unclear about what they're doing and why they're doing it may well descend on them like an avenging angel and usher them disapprovingly to The Appropriate Place. If a child is boisterous in the celebration, they might tell the parent off or, indeed, tell the child off. At meal time, they might hold back politely to allow all the guests to sit down first.

By contrast, a team member who is clear that the main aim is to make strangers feel at home will bear with the parent changing the nappy and gently point out a happier place to do it next time. They will simply smile at the boisterous, disruptive five-year-old and her father and work harder to engage their attention. They will risk being misjudged as greedy when they rush into the meal time and find a seat so that they can sit near the families rather than being part of a holy huddle.

This is why it makes complete sense to spend a moment reminding the team at each meeting of the five values of Messy Church—creativity, celebration, hospitality, all-age and Christ-centred—rather than fretting over details. A team that understands the importance of hospitality cannot help but be hospitable in every move they make. But they need to understand and internalise that identity in order to live it out.

Be good hosts: be generous. It is hard to be generous to a family you've never met if you haven't practised an attitude of generosity within your team. Part of being a good host is to have just such an attitude. Imagine the difference it might make in every team planning meeting and, indeed, every conversation if you all actively and intentionally decided to exercise generosity. It might mean listening to other people's ideas generously. It might mean sharing your own thoughts generously. It might mean applauding when you feel like slapping someone down, or praising when you feel like pouring derision on them. Allow yourselves to be awed by other people. Be wowed by them. Share the riches of your experience and your own personal insights from home, work or school: this is part of the strength of being an intergenerational team.

Be good guests: be willing to receive. Standing in the dynamic space of being both host and guest to each other on our teams, we can also appreciate the value of accepting ideas, resources and insights from others, especially the least likely people—those who might be considered too young or too old, those who have no Christian faith or knowledge that we can tell, or those from other cultures and traditions.

If you have a strong identity, as outlined above, it means you can be good guests to each other and risk opening up to challenges you might otherwise flee. If you are confident that you are a 'Christ-centred' community, for example, you will delight in the fact that a Hindu mum has offered to be on the planning team. As you plan Messy Church sessions together, make a conscious effort to 'receive' from every person on the team at every meeting, making sure that the more vocal people receive from the quieter ones as well as vice versa.

Make others feel that the space is their 'home'. Being part of a planning meeting puts team members into quite a vulnerable position. If I have a good idea for an activity to explore this week's theme, it can take courage to suggest it. I can only do that if I feel I'm in a hospitable and safe space, which feels in some way like home.

Perhaps the overall leader needs to think imaginatively about what would make people feel safer and more at home in the planning meetings, so that fear has no place and every good idea and inspiration can be given an airing. It might mean being more organised about communicating the month's theme in advance so that everybody comes to the meeting having had the opportunity to think and pray about it. It might mean allowing time for personal chat rather than diving straight into business. It might mean using a 'centring' prayer to invite the Holy Spirit to be part of the group and extend her own hospitality to the more timorous members. It might mean taking it in turns to lead the meeting.

Be relational alongside being functional. The apostle Paul was always concerned about the way churches functioned as they grew the kingdom in the first century. He was painfully aware of how easily these small communities could implode or the relationships in them teeter over to the bad, as his letters demonstrate.

It's worth reminding ourselves that, over and over again, Paul comes back to the importance of loving each other, keeping the bigger picture in mind and building strong relationships within an outward- and upward-facing *communitas* (community with a higher purpose). When those core relationships crack, the whole edifice is at risk of crumbling, so love, forgiveness, humility, gentleness, kindness and generosity need to be muscles that are well-exercised every time a team meets. The relationship at the heart of our faith—that happy dance between Father, Son and Holy Spirit, that team which is first and foremost a friendship or a family—is what we should try to emulate in the teams we belong to.

This means we need to put some effort into our relationships and not expect a team meeting, or the delivery of a Messy Church, to be purely functional. There are jobs to be done when we welcome a guest to our house (bed making, spider removal, towel placement), but they exist in order to help us spend time with our guest and enjoy each other's company. Just so, there are jobs to be done to welcome people to a Messy Church and make it the best experience of God they can possibly have. Ultimately, though, the most efficient Messy Church in the world can't be as effective as one in which the team members demonstrate their enormous love for each other, for God and for the outsider. This love needs to be practised at team meetings and in the rest of the community's life during the month.

Know each other and each other's gifts, strengths and weaknesses. Tied in with the importance of good relationships is the part played by knowing each other's strengths and limitations really well. This is part of hospitality, part of recognising how the household works to welcome outsiders. It's a deep curiosity about other people on our team, which affirms that these are people worth taking the trouble to know better. They are interesting people. They must be interesting simply because God made them and made them beautiful, fascinating, intriguing human beings.

It might be appropriate to work through one of the personality tests now available to churches, to gain insights into how you work best together as a team and why everyone reacts as they do to different situations. An in-depth knowledge of each other's strengths and weaknesses will make it easier to back each other up, to know where each other's tipping points are, and to avoid misunderstandings that can be needlessly hurtful.

Face outwards towards new possibilities and people. A hospitable attitude in the team is never inward-facing: it will keep one hand firmly linked to the others already in the group, but the other hand will be stretched out of the circle to draw in outsiders. This is not just about drawing new people on to the team; it's about an attitude of mind that expects to find wisdom in newspapers, on TV, on the web, at the rugby match, at the hairdresser's—places where God is just as much at work as in a church, and possibly more so. A hospitable attitude welcomes new ideas and remains flexible to the risk of trying them out; it refuses to become set in its ways and to assume that the best way is the way it's always been done. It welcomes new ideas as guests and gives them space to see what they might bring to the household.

Put others in the team before yourself, confident that they will put you before themselves. A hospitable attitude means knowing in your heart that you are there to make life better for other people. Your raison d'être is to serve them and give them an environment in which they can flourish, a space that is like the best creative household ever for every single person. While you don't want to end up all falling over yourselves to put the others first ('You choose which activity you'd like to lead'; 'No, you go first'; 'No, please, I insist, you have first pick' and so on), lurking at the back of our minds should always be the thought, 'I don't need to push my agenda; I don't need to stampede over people; I don't need to get my way every time. I know that the others on the team are putting me above themselves, so I can afford to put them above me.'

In our conversations and our planning times, as well as in the delivery of the Messy Church session itself, we should behave like the guest in Jesus' parable and treat each other just as the host treats that guest.

When someone invites you to a wedding feast, do not take the place of honour, for a person more distinguished than you may have been invited. If so, the host who invited both of you will come and say to you, 'Give this person your seat.' Then, humiliated, you will have to take the least important place. But when you are invited, take the lowest place, so that when your host comes, he will say to you,

109

'Friend, move up to a better place.' Then you will be honoured in the presence of all the other guests. For all those who exalt themselves will be humbled, and those who humble themselves will be exalted.
LUKE 14:8–11

We can internally (not out loud—that would be weird) say to each other, 'Friend, move up to a better place,' safe in the knowledge that they will say the same to us. This is true hospitality.

Expect to meet Christ in the others. This is a recurring theme of hospitality. As my team erupt one by one into our hall in a bubble of conversation, coat removal, shoe divesting and dog tickling, ready for our monthly planning meeting, do I really expect to meet Christ in them every time? Do I welcome them as honoured guests? Do I feel privileged to have them under my roof? Am I intentionally listening out for the still small voice of God in the laughter and chatter? Am I tuned in to their body language, preoccupations and behaviour, particularly if it's out of character? Do I care about them enough to bother noticing?

Pitch tents; don't build skyscrapers. Our hospitality as a team is much more like pitching a camp than digging the foundations for a monstrous edifice. We don't have much time together, so we need to create a safe space quickly that will serve as a shelter for our ideas, prayers and plans. We need to remain flexible and light of touch, so that we are always ready to change the way we do things, like being prepared to up sticks and strike the camp or set it up in a different formation. One of the dangers of established church is that it can invite people to get in a rut and allow traditions to fossilise into immovable edifices that suffocate anything new. Messy Church has the chance to stay flexible, like an army camp that is ready to move on at the blast of a trumpet. Hospitality might mean not being stuck in our ways, leaving a space at the planning table for the outsider, inviting less comfortable people to join us, even when that disturbs our cosy, efficiently running clique.

Commit to the long haul. Alongside this lightness of touch and flexibility of structure, there is a need to commit to our aims for a length of time and not just to opt out when the going gets tough. Hospitality isn't easy (although it gets easier with practice), and, for the sake of the strong household identity, it requires a certain component of the team who will stick with it through discouragements as well as through happy times. This is good practice for more extreme forms of hospitality, such as opening up homes to needy people or intentionally turning our whole church into a community that is focused not only on God but on the outsider, but a Messy Church team needs that same commitment.

Enjoy it; if you don't, find ways to enjoy it. What energises you? What do you look forward to? What do you enjoy? I firmly believe that one aspect of hospitality is that there is joy alongside the sacrifice. It should be a joy to be hospitable to each other, and, if it's not, perhaps it's worth thinking imaginatively about how to make your team more enjoyable to belong to. The small investment of bringing cake to a planning meeting (or a bottle of wine or a tasty snack to nibble), having a nice craft or game to try out together, filming a simple video of your last Messy Church and watching it together over popcorn, laughing over photos, playing an extract from the *Messy Church* DVD to talk about, going for a short walk on a beautiful evening to collect natural items to use in an activity—all these are imaginative touches that can turn a dull meeting into a real treat, shot through with fun.

Expect it to be messy: relax into it, embrace it, enjoy it. Hospitality is always going to be about risk, adventure and unpredictability. As soon as we open our doors to this attitude of mind, we can expect things to get messier rather than neater. This is something to celebrate and embrace and look forward to rather than to panic about. We don't need to be in control. God is in control; it's his party and we are all guests. We can treat our planning meetings more like a party than a duty; we can be frivolous and let our silly imaginations run riot because, as a team, we have created a strong identity, a common purpose with clear values, a tent with infinitely expandable walls. This in itself will be so attractive that those on the outside will long to belong. (A woman can dream…)

Add your own insights. What other opportunities do you see to have hospitality infiltrating and shaping the way you work together as a team?

QUESTIONS

- Keep reminding yourselves of your household identity. What are the five Messy Church values? What are the values of your own church?

- Be good hosts: be generous. Who do you know who is 'hospitably generous' in the way they converse with you?

- Be good guests: be willing to receive. Are there any groups of people that you feel are under-represented on your team?

- Make others feel that the space is their 'home'. Which of the suggestions relating to this point would be useful in your context?

- Be relational alongside being functional. How well do you know each other? Do the newcomers feel as included as the people who have been in the team longer?

- Know each other and each other's gifts, strengths and weaknesses. Play the game of sending round pieces of paper, each with the name of one person in your team, and writing on them what you think the person's strengths are.

- Face outwards towards new possibilities and people. When was the last time you deliberately did something edgy as a team?

- Put others in the team before yourself. Read Luke 14:8–11 together. What do you think is the most important point in this parable?

- Expect to meet Christ in the others. What difference would there be in the way you met if Christ was there in person?

- Pitch tents; don't build skyscrapers. Are there any bad habits that are gradually solidifying in your Messy Church?

- Commit to the long haul. Celebrate the people who have been on the team since the beginning: show your gratitude with a card or a bunch of flowers.

- Enjoy it; if you don't, find ways to enjoy it. Do you each enjoy making your Messy Church happen?

- Expect it to be messy: relax into it, embrace it, enjoy it. How can your planning meetings be 'more like a party than a duty'?

- What are your insights?

CHAPTER 7

TEAM TRAINING SESSION ON HOSPITALITY

Before the session, ask everyone to go to a building, business or public gathering where they've never been before, and to observe how they are made to feel welcome or unwelcome. Ask them to note down exactly what made them feel that way.

As the team arrives for the session, have someone (not the leader) hosting, who should make a point of giving a deliberately brilliant welcome. Include as many of the following points as you can, and any more you can think of:

- Make sure the event has been clearly publicised in plenty of time to the right people.

- Make the entrance to the building very obvious.

- Make parking provision very obvious.

- Point out toilets, disabled toilet, exits and nappy changing facilities as people arrive.

- Greet everyone by name and warmly within the bounds of appropriateness for your cultural context.

- Offer them a drink and snack.

- Make it clear where they are invited to sit.

- Have programmes around with the evening's timetable set out in English, any other first languages spoken by the team (or any language, just to make a point), and in diagrammatic form for pre-readers.

- Make sure each person is linked up with someone else: 'Sid, did you know Jan has an allotment just like yours?'

Pray to welcome God into this group of his people. Then introduce the evening as an opportunity to explore hospitality in your Messy Church.

Ask the group what they can remember about the way they were welcomed just now. What words or actions of welcome do they remember? Was there anything special about the way the welcoming space was set up? What about the pre-meeting hospitality? Was the invitation hospitable? How, exactly? How did the welcome make them feel?

Enjoy watching clips from one or two comedies that show challenging customer service: the Channel 4 series *Black Books* is a great source, as is the BBC's *Fawlty Towers* or *Miranda* (especially the scene where Miranda is in the shop as customers arrive).

If there is time, you could divide into groups of no more than five, and use whatever materials you have to hand to create a model of the most powerful symbol of hospitality you can think of. Bring the models together and talk them through.

Alternatively, divide into two groups and, if possible, go into different spaces to discuss and rehearse. Ask both groups to prepare the most inhospitable welcome possible, to your particular building. Give them five minutes to prepare, then ask each group to act out the scenario, using the other group as their 'guests'.

(Any rudeness *should* be mitigated by the fact that everyone knows it's a game, but make sure everyone has a proper debrief in case anyone's feelings have been inadvertently hurt.) Analyse what went into the appalling welcomes and how you were all made to feel.

Read Luke 7:36–50 (the account of Jesus as a guest in Simon the Pharisee's house). Talk briefly about how you all picture the scene—the walls, the furniture, the people present, the smells, the sorts of food on the table, and so on. Discuss the following questions.

- Who had most power in this situation? Why?

- Who had least power? Why?

- How would you describe Jesus' behaviour as a guest? Does that raise any challenges for us as a church?

- What would you say was the main problem with Simon's hospitality? Does that raise any challenges for us in our welcome as a church?

- What would you say was the best thing about the woman's hospitality? Does that raise any challenges for us as a church?

- Is there anything else that strikes you about hospitality from this account?

Talk about the experiences of hospitality that the group has had in their pre-session visit to somewhere unfamiliar.

Focus on your Messy Church. Divide into four groups and give each group the task of discussing a particular 'zone' of Messy Church: the welcome, the activity time, the celebration or the meal. Give them the questions at the end of Chapters 1–4, appropriate to their group. Take 20 minutes to talk them through.

Come back together and summarise the results. Make sure the conclusions are communicated with the whole team and the church afterwards.

CHAPTER 8

LEARNING FROM THE HOSPITALITY INDUSTRY

As we've been exploring, part of hospitality (and, frankly, part of common sense) is to be ready to learn from the outsider—the host learning from the guest and accepting wisdom wherever it comes from, if it really is wisdom. If we, as churches, assume the role of host on the rather shaky ground that *we got there first*, what can we learn from a hospitality industry that now operates well away from church?

Hospitality has moved on from its roots in the homes of the first-century followers of the Way, who made their homes safe bases for itinerant preachers and apostles in an age when commercial inns were dirty and dangerous. It's now a multimillion-pound industry, the fourth largest industry in the UK according to the British Hospitality Association, employing more than 2.6 million people across the UK. We're talking about holiday accommodation of different sorts, from campsites to hotels, places to eat and drink, catering services for organisations and event hospitality: the industry is huge. One in every 14 jobs is in hospitality and tourism, according to the *State of the Nation Report 2013* produced by the industries charity People 1st. This is a far cry from the amateur provision made by Benedict at his monasteries: this is professionalisation big-time.

As an aside, it's worth pondering the way hospitality (rather than mere 'service' or 'commerce', which are simply about treating food and shelter as purchasable commodities), education and health provision in the West have all started from small, inspired, compassionate Christian roots, based on Jesus' concern for people of all degrees of poverty and social status to have life in all its fullness. These concerns have become embedded in society, made professional, state-run and systematic. This is obviously a good thing but it does leave room for the 'subsidiarity' that Justin Welby described—the personal, amateur heartbeat of hospitality, health and education working alongside the professional systems. The Hospitality Guild website suggests reasons for joining the industry: it is 'exciting... sociable... dynamic' and offers 'variety' and 'comparatively fast career progression'. This says nothing about bringing joy to others, sheltering the needy or making strangers feel at home. It is all about the benefits that the industry brings to its employees—hardly an ideological inspiration. Perhaps we amateurs have a role to play in reminding the huge monster of the hospitality industry what its roots are and how it has the potential to transform lives, as well as encouraging its employees to go into it for less self-centred reasons.

THE IMPORTANCE OF AN ONLINE PRESENCE

The People 1st report on the hospitality industry highlights trends for the future. One trend that we in the church can learn from is the increased importance of social media and an online presence as the new 'reception desk' or first port of call. Here, more than in any other sphere, we need to let those who are digital natives show us the way. It's been a great blessing to us to have members of the BRF Messy Church team who are in their early 20s and happily tweet without the raised blood pressure, shortage of breath and breakout of cold sweat that Twitter still provokes from me, a Generation X-er.

It's no good laughing off these technological advances and hoping they will go away: the digital world is here to stay and the problem for many churches is that the people who are in decision-making roles are often not digital natives and do not use the internet for everyday living in the same way that millennials do. Our websites, Twitter feeds and Facebook pages are the equivalent of the noticeboard outside our church and half a dozen town criers employed to shout out what's on in church this week; they are as crucial as (even more crucial than!) the parish magazine; they are a vital part of hospitality at the level of simply letting everybody know we exist and that they are welcome.

I tried to visit a Messy Church on a recent holiday outside my own area. Sadly, their registration on our directory was out of date, their website hadn't been updated for so long that I didn't trust it to contain reliable information, the church and surrounding benefice churches had no other references on Google, and the email contact that I found belonged to someone who happened to be away on holiday. By the time they replied to my email query, it was too late. That didn't desperately matter for me, but what if I'd been a lonely family or individual wanting to join that Messy Church—or, indeed, that church? We need to sit at the feet of our teenagers and 20-somethings if we are not confident about technology ourselves, and we need to prioritise our web presence in our budgets. Paul wrote in Romans 10:14, 'How, then, can they call on the one they have not believed in? And how can they believe in the one of whom they have not heard? And how can they hear without someone preaching to them?' Perhaps today he would write, 'How can they know about your church without somebody taking the trouble to maintain a lively online presence? Because that is where the younger generations spend most of their time.'

IMPORTANCE OF THE SKILLS NEEDED TO MAKE HOSPITALITY WORK

The People 1st report also identifies the industry's overwhelming belief that 'customer service skills' are the most necessary, followed by management and leadership skills. I took the Hospitality Guild personality test (www. hospitalityguild.co.uk/A-Career-in-Hospitality/Personality-

Test) to see what roles would suit me best in the hospitality industry. Apparently I would be an excellent Tour Guide or Entertainments Team Manager. This figures: I happily see myself as the Entertainments Manager for the variously gifted Messy Church team at BRF (mostly because their idea of entertainment is delivering a superlative Messy Church session and seeing people come close to God through it), and being a Tour Guide seems an eminently apt way of describing the Messy pilgrimage we're all on. But the emphasis on the *type* of people needed by the hospitality industry, rather than the *hard skills* they have, is significant. The Restaurant Schools website says, in its 'Top Ten Qualities of a Great Hospitality Employee': 'To be successful in hospitality, one must have top notch interpersonal skills, as the very nature of the business is to provide spectacular customer service.' In fact, in their Top Ten list, the only 'hard skills' mentioned are computer know-how and knowledge of health and safety issues; the other qualities are about the sort of person required—committed, enthusiastic, thorough and so on.

For us in churches, our primary requirement is not for people to have hard skills in theology, sport, craft, team management or administration, useful though these are; what we need more than anything is a team of people, committed to Christ, whose characters are growing ever more Christ-like. There are certain aspects of Christ-like living that can be learnt formally, but it is mostly about character. If we have a deep-seated desire to serve others and serve God, we will do the right thing by instinct more than because we've been well-trained. In a restaurant we visited as a family recently, the waiter was outgoing and friendly because that was his very nature: he didn't need to be taught to be so. (He could, however, have used some specific customer services training to avoid using phrases like 'Well, guys and girls…!' to a group of customers including someone with feminist leanings who was old enough to be his mother and someone else who has strong views about gender-binary reinforcement.)

The most helpful and inspiring resource I have discovered from the hospitality industry is the book *Setting the Table* by Danny Meyer (Marshall Cavendish, 2010). In this book (half autobiography, half secrets-of-the-industry), he describes how he started and continues to run his chain of successful New York restaurants. Apart from the obvious drive, joy, passion and mission of the man himself, which shine from every page, he keeps coming back to certain principles that he believes have made his businesses successful. It's well worth checking out his talks on YouTube. Here are ten of his principles, which I think are thought-provoking for us in our quest to provide insightful Christian hospitality in and out of church. There are so many more I could usefully explore—read the book!

1. 'Put hospitality to work first for the people who work for me… then our guests, community, suppliers and investors' (p. 2). I was surprised and intrigued by this insight. It's not Meyer's customers who are the first to be treated hospitably; it's his staff. Churches can learn from this: let's encourage each other, praise each other, inspire, challenge, equip and mentor each other. Let's welcome our guests, yes, but let's create or affirm an ethos of welcoming every member of our team too. Some of the most inspiring Messy Church leaders

I've encountered are brilliant at this—greeting every team member affectionately by name, taking the time to show a personal interest in them, making sure they have everything they need to do the job, encouraging them during the session, noticing the things they do and thanking them afterwards.

2. 'What's most meaningful is creating positive uplifting outcomes for human experiences and human relationships' (p. 4). Meyer sees right through to the heart of hospitality. It's not just about providing a fabulous service to the guests; it's much more about making a space where great encounters can happen, where friendships are grown and where wholesome, life-enhancing experiences can take place. The actual activities, celebration and meal we provide in Messy Churches, at one level, simply make space for great relationship-building and friendship-making across the generations. Henri Nouwen writes:

Hospitality means primarily the creation of free space where the stranger can enter and become a friend instead of an enemy. Hospitality is not to change people, but to offer them space where change can take place. It is not to bring men and women over to our side, but to offer freedom not disturbed by dividing lines.
REACHING OUT (BANTAM DOUBLEDAY DELL, 2000)

3. '[Hospitality] is present when something happens for you. It is absent when something happens to you' (p. 11). How often are we guilty of 'delivering a programme' to our passive consumerist guests? Hospitality, rather than 'service', is about something much more mutual. It embraces the idea that our guests have experience, wisdom and challenge to

bring to the worship space; young and old, we are all both givers and receivers.

4. 'If you're trying to provide engaging hospitality and outstanding technical service, there must also be a certain amount of fun' (p. 51). I am, I admit, slightly obsessive about championing the need to have fun in church, to be joyful as much as we are solemn (if not slightly more joyful than solemn, especially when we are working on the edges, as we are in Messy Church). We need to enjoy this ministry and be engaged with the experiences and the people. We need to look forward to it with gleeful anticipation and look back on it fondly. The best Messy Churches are those in which the team is enjoying itself as much as the guests. When we enjoy it too, it stops being a duty that we solemnly carry out for others and starts being a pleasure and a privilege to relish for ourselves—one that nurtures us, not just the guests.

5. 'Hospitality is the sum of all the thoughtful, caring gracious things our staff does to make you feel we are on your side' (p. 65). Maybe this sums up hospitality—that we are all on the same side. You have come to church expecting to have a good (engaging, challenging, numinous, instructive, relational, moving) time with your children or grandchildren or extended family; we, the team, delight in using our creativity and financial resources to enable that to happen. It's what church is for us. If you are in an unconventional family set-up, does the church team make you feel you belong or does it make you feel you are not quite up to the mark? If you have particular needs, maybe a

disability, does the church team enjoy finding a way to give you full access to everything on offer, or are you made to feel a bit of a nuisance?

6. 'Always be collecting dots' (p. 80). This is very challenging for me, as a somewhat happy-go-lucky busker of all things administrative. The 'dots' Meyer refers to are items of information about his customers. Even before the days of computers, he made a point of collecting and storing information about regular customers so that he could 'connect the dots' or give them a surprisingly personal experience, based on what he knew about them. This might sound really creepy to us Brits, but it is actually a way of showing how much you care—for example, remembering birthdays and anniversaries, deciding which people might get on with another family because they have something in common, or encouraging a family to help with a particular activity because you heard them say what experts they are in a particular field. One of our teenagers is a Scout and a pyromaniac. We have only done two Messy Churches so far, but I'm looking forward to the session that lends itself to fire. (Perhaps I should say that those on the team who know him better have more reservations.)

Collecting, sharing and storing appropriate information that, used sensitively, can help us connect people and show our care is, overall, a great principle. We obviously need to be careful about data protection and confidentiality, but caring enough to have a birthday card ready can insult no one.

7. 'At its best, a restaurant should not let guests leave without feeling as though they've been satisfyingly hugged' (p. 87). Don't you just love this? Let's rephrase it: 'At its best, a church should not let its members leave without feeling as though they've been satisfyingly hugged.' We have the best hugger in history as our God, if we take the parable of the prodigal father seriously—the dad who stripped off all his dignity, ran to his disgraceful son and flung his arms round him in an act of totally shocking acceptance, grace, forgiveness and cultural norm-defying love. Philippians 2 comes to mind again, doesn't it?

When did you last see a church's mission statement that declared, 'No one will leave this church without feeling they've been satisfyingly hugged'? In our Western society, where isolation or loneliness is one of the biggest problems for the elderly, and where lack of real human contact among the young is raising concern for their emotional development, making a church a gathering where everyone feels that, at some level, they have been satisfyingly and appropriately hugged is a jolly good, entirely holy and theologically robust aspiration. We can hug with the way we listen. We can hug with eye contact. We can hug with an encircling prayer. We can reveal the God who longs to throw his arms around all his children. And, where appropriate, we can provide the physical, very human reassurance and comfort that is a hug. It might be the only one that person gets this month.

8. 'Hire people to whom caring for others is in fact a selfish act: "hospitalarians"' (p. 146). Meyer wants to employ people whose delight is in caring for others, whose energy

comes from caring for others, who are distressed if they are prevented from caring for others. Notice that his phrase is not 'serving'; it is 'caring for'. True hospitality leaves service far behind: the service comes naturally and logically from the joy of caring for people. These 'hospitalarians' are the people who need to be at the door of your Messy Church. They need to be at every activity table. They need to be on the cooks' team. Frankly, the whole team needs to be made up of people who are either already hospitalarians or who only need a bit of encouragement to reveal their inner hospitalarian. They need the language, actions and excuse to start doing what they already know in their heart is part of their identity. Maybe they've been taught to disapprove of certain people, certain groups or certain behaviours— but churches have too many disapproving people. Let's give them a chance to reveal their inner hospitalarian. And if that inner hospitalarian has become so stifled that it has actually died, let's bid them a gentle farewell and let them use their gifts in God's service elsewhere. Messy Church is so exhausting that we need people who will be fed by it, not sapped by it with no reward.

9. 'Enlightened hospitality works best with optimistic, hope-ful open-minded people at the helm. It tends not to work when the leaders are sceptics who think they already have all the answers' (p. 206). Now here's a challenge for our churches! As we look for leaders and ministers, and as we select them for training, are we on the look-out for these opti-mistic, hopeful and open-minded people, or do we despise them as naïve, childish and immature? There is so much to be gloomy about in the Western church today that we may

be tempted to despise those who advocate hope. It seems like the option for the stupid. But Meyer knows that successful hospitality needs a positive, expectant, excited attitude to guide it, to see the new opportunities, to keep pressing on into the unknown. Let's treasure our hopeful leaders in the church. Let's follow them rather than the doom-merchants, or we risk falling into self-fulfilling prophecies.

10. 'Hospitality is hopeful; it is confident, thoughtful, optimistic, generous and openhearted' (p. 207). 'God is hopeful; he is confident, thoughtful, optimistic, generous and openhearted.' Can you also say the following?

- My team is hopeful; we are confident, thoughtful, optimistic, generous and openhearted.
- My church is...
- My home is...
- I am...

The Good Hospitality Services Inc. website includes among its core values one value that takes us aback—us nice shepherds of the sheep, us nice Christian people doing a nice Christian thing nicely: 'We will always be determined to be an industry leader that is led through our aggressive and innovative approach to the hospitality industry.'

While some of us panic at the thought of being 'aggressive' and 'determined', let's not refuse these traits point blank. Let's, at the very least, be purposeful and intentional in our hospitality. We can't assume that it will happen all by itself with no effort on our part. We need to allow that aggressive side of our personalities or teams to give an energy to our Messy Churches, making them the most hospitable spaces they can be.

QUESTIONS

- What made your last visit to a restaurant, café or hotel a good or bad example of hospitality?
- What can you draw from this that will help your hospitality at Messy Church?

CHAPTER 9

BOUNDARIES

While clear boundaries are essential for the sort of hospitality that involves welcoming people to your community to stay, there is more flexibility in Messy Church. Boundaries for us, who may only meet as a gathered community once a month, are more about a very strong centre and deliberately messy edges. They are about a gravitational pull rather than fencing off or building walls. We can cope with messy behaviour for a mere two hours: that's very different from living with people 24/7, where house rules are much more important. Like the heavenly city in Revelation 21, the gates of Messy Churches stand open. But unlike the heavenly city, there are no angels making sure 'nothing impure will ever enter it, nor will anyone who does what is shameful or deceitful, but only those whose names are written in the Lamb's book of life' (v. 27). We will need this purity when we're living with each other for eternity, but we don't need it for two hours a month. The angels at the door of a Messy Church are indiscriminate and welcome in people who have only just started to discover where their name is written.

Would we turn anyone away? Yes: I would (kindly) turn away a child coming on their own. I would make sure I was operating in an accountable system, with someone present who knows about those who need to stay away from children because of their criminal records. In the unlikely event of someone coming through the door under the influence of drugs or alcohol, or with an obvious intent to harm or destroy, I would find a way of turning them around. But I can't think of anyone else I would refuse entry to. Can you? Have you?

SAFEGUARDING

This is the safeguarding advice we offer on our website.

We all have a responsibility to safeguard and promote the welfare of children and young people, even if we don't have a specific safeguarding role.

It can be an easy mistake to think that because parents and carers are present when you hold a group or an activity, safeguarding isn't really necessary. To some degree, you will be viewed as being in 'a position of trust'.

The majority of Messy Churches operate under the authority of a local church, and therefore should be covered by the Safeguarding Policy of that church or denomination. Check this with your church or denomination to make sure. You will need to identify the appointed Safeguarding Officer of your church or denomination, make yourself known to them and share their contact details with those involved with running/leading your Messy Church. It is a good idea to ask if they could arrange some Safeguarding Training for anyone supporting or working with families.

Messy Churches need to comply with legislation and government expectations with regards to safeguarding. Where abuse is disclosed, witnessed or suspected, it needs to be reported to the statutory authorities (Children's Social Care or the police). However, you should discuss this with those responsible for safeguarding, either at your church or within your denomination.

- Be prepared to challenge unsafe practice or inappropriate behaviour by adults.
- Record your concerns and share them with relevant people as soon as you can.
- You may need to act/respond within a short timescale — think about whether a child may be at risk of immediate harm.
- Have a list of contact names and numbers for people to report any concerns to.
- Trust your judgement: if something doesn't seem right then act appropriately.

It is our responsibility to provide a safe place for our families to meet, where children should not knowingly be put at risk of significant harm.

If you need to respond to a concern quickly, without the opportunity to speak to your designated Safeguarding Officer, then contact your local authority Children's Social Care Services, the police or NSPCC Child Protection Helpline 0808 800 5000 (24-hour). For more information talk to the person responsible for Safeguarding in your church or denomination (your minister should be able to advise how to get in touch with them).

Another valuable source of help and information is CCPAS (www.ccpas.org.uk).

We also put the question about safeguarding to our Facebook community, and here are the responses:

We insist that everyone attends our safeguarding training and strongly encourage all helpers to apply for a DBS, but, as parents/ family are responsible for children throughout, we cannot make it a three-line whip—though that may happen in time. The team are very good, though, and are usually willing to do both, and most of them already have a DBS and have attended training in another capacity.

Here are the procedures we follow at our Messy Church:
- *All leaders must undergo a 'Working with Children Check' and attend a training course.*
- *All children must be accompanied and supervised by a responsible adult at all times.*
- *Parents are to advise us of any allergies.*

We take safeguarding seriously at our Messy Church. Every team member has a signed volunteer agreement, and has attended the safeguarding module and completed DBS checks. All paperwork is filed with the church safeguarding officer. New team members have to provide two references and have an interview with the safer recruitment team before going through the procedure above.

At our church, all of our Messy Church leaders possess a Blue Card, which is a volunteer child worker police safety check. Each family entering must register with all safety disclosed and signed consent given for photography.

Some dioceses suggest an online safeguarding course.

BOUNDARIES IN THE KITCHEN

We want to keep people safe and well. This means preparing and serving food hygienically and with an awareness of local and national guidance. Messy Churches operate across so many countries and so many authorities that BRF cannot offer guidance that will apply at all times and in all places.

I wrote to the UK Food Standards Authority in 2015 and received this reply, which may be helpful:

For an activity to require registration, it must have 'a certain continuity of activities' and 'a certain degree of organisation'. The occasional provision of food, for example, at an office working lunch or charity event is unlikely to constitute food business activity. Food Hygiene certificates are not required. Those providing the food, however, should make every effort to ensure that the food is safe to eat.

The interpretation of the phrase 'a certain continuity of activities', which is contained in European food hygiene legislation, should help organisers of community and charity events who want to provide food. It should also help local authority food safety officers decide whether or not to register activities carried out in the village hall, community and charity sector.

The FSA suggests that, generally, providing food less than once a month is not considered to have 'a certain continuity of activities'. In describing 'degree of organisation' we have emphasised the importance of the complexity of the food safety controls, vulnerability of consumers and size of event in consideration against continuity.

The guidance includes a number of general examples to

help illustrate the Agency's interpretation of 'continuity' and 'organisation', although these examples will not cover all circumstances.

The guidance will be reviewed and updated, as necessary. The guidance, and information about FSA Red Tape Challenge initiatives, can be found via the links below: http://food.gov.uk/news-updates/news/2013/jul/halls.

The agency's advice to anyone providing food for such events is to get in touch with their local environmental health department. To find your local council please go to: www.food.gov.uk/enforcement/yourarea.

A rule of thumb for most Messy Churches is to have a team who have undergone training in a Basic Food Hygiene course (available online or through a local college). There is often somebody who has catered professionally in some capacity and works to a high standard because of their training. At the time of writing, in the UK it is required (and is an aspect of thoughtful hospitality) to keep a record of all ingredients used in the meal and to display on a sign any ingredients that might trigger one of the common allergies.

RISK ASSESSMENTS

You will find a sample risk assessment form on the Messy Church website (www.messychurch.org.uk/resource/messy-church-risk-assessment). They are challenging to fill in but very useful: they allow you to welcome people into a space where risks can be taken, because those risks have been assessed and necessary safety procedures put in place.

MESSY CHURCH SESSIONS ON HOSPITALITY

SESSION 1

ABRAHAM AND THE THREE VISITORS

Aim: to see how offering hospitality gives back to you far more than you give out: if you bless others through hospitality, you will be blessed

Bible reference: Genesis 18:1–15

ACTIVITIES

1. BUILD A CAMP

You will need: sheets; tarpaulins; blankets; clothes pegs; ropes; clothes horses; chairs; tables; pop-up tents

Invite each family to make a tent as part of a Messy campsite. You could build the tents where you normally hold the celebration and lead it with everyone sitting in or near a tent.

Talk about the lifestyle of Abraham: he and his extended family left their houses in Ur and travelled around, living in tents, following God's call.

2. GREAT TREES

You will need: watercolour paper; paintbrushes; watercolour paints; water spray bottle

Using a brush, drop small blobs of colour on to the paper in a very rough triangle shape. Spray a fine mist of water over the blobs to make them run into interesting shapes. Paint in a trunk and branches with a brush. (You will find full instructions and tutorials on this kind of activity if you search 'autumn colours tree' on Pinterest.com.)

Talk about the way Abraham and Sarah made their camp near the great trees at Mamre and how the trees would give them and their visitors shade from the hot sun.

3. THREE VISITORS

You will need: a printed copy of Genesis 18:1–2; copies of artists' interpretations of this scene (search Google Images for 'Abraham's visitors'); art materials

Make a picture of what you think the arrival of the three visitors was like. What was the weather like? What did the countryside look like? What were the travellers wearing? Were they carrying anything? Were they old, young, men, women or children? What colour skin did they have? What sort of mood were they in?

Talk about what a strange and unexpected arrival this was for Abraham.

4. FOOT SPA

You will need: a foot spa machine if someone can lend you one, or bowls, water, lotions and oils of whatever sort you have available; peppermint foot spray; towels; comfy chairs

Encourage people to give their friend or family member a refreshing foot pamper session, or offer to do it yourself.

Talk about what you do to welcome people when they come into your house for a drink or a barbecue or to stay. In Abraham's time, and in Jesus' time a lot later, the way to welcome someone as an honoured guest was to wash their dusty feet.

5. WELCOME MINI-SNACK BOWLS

You will need: baking trays for cupcakes; spray-on cooking fat; meltable beads (the sort you usually iron); baking paper (for naming); paper serviettes; oven; snacks, such as seeds, grapes and crisps

Spray the tray with fat to prevent sticking. Fill a 'cupcake mould' in the baking tray with a single layer of beads, going across the base of the mould and up the sides, as high as possible without tumbling out. Bake in a hot oven (200°C, Gas 6) for ten minutes. Leave to cool and prise out. Place a piece of paper serviette inside and fill with a healthy welcoming snack.

Talk about the way you welcome people: sometimes it's nice to offer a drink and a snack when they arrive, especially if they've been travelling. Abraham wanted to give the best he had to offer to his visitors. Perhaps you can offer visitors to your house something from your bowl to make them welcome.

6. CHEESY SNACKERELS

You will need: crackers; soft cheese; grapes; chopping board; knives (in addition, milk, salt and vinegar to make your own soft cheese)

Make a welcoming snack for someone else: spread soft cheese on a cracker and top with half a grape. Share immediately.

Alternatively, if you feel adventurous, you could make your own soft cheese. Heat milk, with salt, to 87.7°C, add vinegar to curdle it and wait for the curds to drip-drain for 15 minutes. This involves several stages and a lot of waiting, so it would be difficult to do as an ongoing activity, but you might find a whey (sorry) to do it safely—maybe as a spectator sport with a responsible adult doing the hot bits. Recipes can be found on the internet.

Talk about the meal Abraham and Sarah made for the three visitors. They offered them bread, cheese and roast meat—a real feast. Who makes you welcome with a feast? Why do you think we eat together at Messy Church?

7. MORNINGS OF JOY

You will need: copies of Psalm 30:5 ('Weeping may stay for the night, but rejoicing comes in the morning'); circles of card or paper plates for younger people; hole punch; thread; collage scraps

On one side of the card circle, write (or stick on) the phrase 'Weeping may stay for the night' and, on the other side, 'But rejoicing comes in the morning'. Decorate the two sides of the card with scraps, in colours that represent sadness on one side and joy on the other. Punch a hole in the top and thread a piece of thread through to hang it up.

An older person's version of this activity might be to marble the two different sides in different coloured marbling inks, allow to dry and write over the top with a Sharpie pen.

Sarah and Abraham had been very sad for a very long time as they didn't have children, but they trusted that their lives were in God's hands and that he had a plan for them. Talk about how sad times can be a very hard 'night' to go through, but if our lives, like theirs, are in God's hands, there will always be a joyful 'morning' in the end. For Sarah and Abraham, this came when they showed hospitality.

8. VINTAGE WELCOME SIGN

You will need: rough planks of wood of any size (big is more fun, but small is more welcomed by parents); drill; sandpaper; paint; blackboard paint; chalk or other colouring equipment; stencils of the letters for WELCOME; cord or string

Sand down your plank until it's still rough but not actually splintery. Drill holes for cord to hang it by. Paint it if desired or leave the wood showing. (You might decide to do some ready-made ones up to this point, for smaller people.) Use the stencils to turn it into a vintage-chic welcome sign to go outside your door, and add a cord hanger. It could hang vertically or horizontally or simply be propped up against a wall.

9. BASICS BANK COLLECTION

You will need: a selection of items needed by your local food bank or basics bank; a guest; leaflets

Invite somebody who helps at the basics bank to come and talk informally to families about what happens at the basics bank and how their work helps families. Ask them to talk particularly about how this work expresses the hospitality of the local churches, shops and other community groups. As conversations go on, younger people could be asked to choose which ten items they think would be most useful for a family to have in a bag to take away.

10. WELCOME POT

You will need: terracotta flowerpots; compost; plants; acrylic paints; sticky letters

Decorate a plant pot with the paints and write or stick the word 'welcome' on one side. Plant up with compost and a plant and invite people to leave their pot near their front door.

Talk about the cost of welcoming people to your home, in time, food and effort. In Jesus' economy (the kingdom of God), the payback is *huge*!

(You could invite people to pay a small sum for this craft, to raise money for BRF's continued Messy work.)

CELEBRATION

STORY

Have everybody sitting or lying in their tents if desired. Tell the story as if you're all sitting round a campfire. Jesus would have loved this story, as it was the story of his great-great-great-great-great- (times lots and lots) grandpa and grandma.

It was very hot. Abraham and Sarah (anyone here called Sarah?) were very old... and a bit sad because they really wanted children and they didn't have any. And as Abraham sat in the shade in the hottest part of the day, he suddenly saw something surprising:

three strangers had popped up out of nowhere! Did he shut his eyes and hope they went away? No! Did he leave someone else to welcome them? No! Did he give them a crust of bread and tell them to go away? No! He dashed out and bowed low and welcomed them in and sat them down and washed their feet. Sarah made loads of bread and they roasted a cow and they made a yummy milk-shakey, cheesy sort of drink, and they gave the three visitors the best welcome meal they possibly could!

As they welcomed the visitors and made them feel at home, they realised that those three strangers were really angels sent by God. Maybe one of them was even God himself! The angels were happy because they had seen that this was a family that would teach all its members to give the best welcome ever to anyone in need. They promised that by the time they came back, Sarah would have a baby after all!

Sarah did have a baby, called Isaac (anyone here called Isaac?), and he had children and they had children, and in the end Jesus was born into the same family. And the Bible says that God has adopted all of us into his family too, through Jesus. So, that welcome from Abraham and Sarah meant that a special baby could be welcomed to the family, which meant that Jesus could be welcomed to earth, which meant that we can be welcomed into God's amazing family. What amazing things happen when we show hospitality, when we welcome strangers as if they are family!

PRAYER

Stand up and hold your arms out to one side with palms together. Say, 'Jesus, sometimes our lives are like closed doors.'

Now open your arms so that one arm is sticking out at either side. Say, 'Thank you that you died on the cross so that the door to heaven is open to anyone who wants to come in.'

Now put your hands slightly forwards as if you're welcoming someone. Say, 'Help us to be like Abraham and Sarah and to welcome other people into our life and our home, into your church and your kingdom.'

SESSION 2

THE MEALS JESUS ATE

Aim: to understand more of how Jesus loved and accepted absolutely everybody, and showed his acceptance by eating with them

Bible reference: Matthew 9:9–12

ACTIVITIES

1. MENU BOARDS

You will need: pieces of plywood (or very strong card) roughly A5 size, enough for one on each table at the Messy meal time, and blackboard paint (or small blackboards from a cheap stationer's); liquid chalk pens; wooden blocks with a slot in to act as a stand if desired

You could paint the boards with blackboard paint and let them dry beforehand. Then decorate around the edges of the blackboards and use them as menus on the tables for each Messy Church.

Talk about why we put on a meal at Messy Church—because we want to be like Jesus and welcome everybody to sit down and get to know each other and him better.

2. SERVIETTE FOLDING

You will need: good-quality and cheap paper serviettes

Search on the internet for 'serviette folding' until you find a design you feel confident to learn. A waterlily or a swan might be a good start. Encourage people to practise on the cheap serviettes and then to make a really good one for the Messy meal out of a better-quality serviette.

Talk about welcoming people to come and eat in Messy Church and, if the conversation goes that way, in our own homes too. Why do we do it? Because Jesus loved eating with people and we do too. Can you think of any meals he ate with people?

3. HOSPITALITY IN A JAR

You will need: clean glass jars; the ingredients from www.bbcgoodfood.com/recipes/956638/ chocolate-brownie-mix-in-a-jar; labels with the instructions printed on them

Invite the families to make up the jar full of the ingredients, then take it home, make the brownies and invite someone else to come and eat with them.

You might prefer to make soup in a jar or noodles in a jar instead: recipes are easily found online to suit your budget. A good source of inspiration is http://inhabitat.com/diy-gift-idea-10-recipes-you-can-gift-in-jars.

Talk about who you might invite and whether there is someone you could invite who never gets invited to things and who will probably never invite you back. Families could take a photo of themselves making and then enjoying the food and post it on your Facebook page.

4. SIEVING AND SORTING

You will need: an assortment of sieves, colanders and other things with holes; different materials to sift (for example, pebbles, beads, sand, flour, out-of-date pulses and beans, dry compost); bowls

Have fun with the different textures, mixing them up and trying to sort and sift the materials into separate piles.

(You could make this a useful activity instead, by sorting a box of junk bits and bobs into usable heaps. You could sort out crayons that need sharpening, pens that don't work any more, mixtures of drawing pins and paper clips, and so on.)

Talk about how we sometimes select or sort the kind of people we are happy to welcome as friends and 'sieve out' the rest, but Jesus had no 'sieve': he welcomed everybody.

5. WELCOME/UNWELCOME TO MY TABLE

You will need: magazines with pictures of all sorts of people of all ages, cultures, races, genders, personalities and occupations; pictures of different tables, labelled as daringly as you like (for example, church table, Jesus' table, my table at home, my classroom desk, my office desk, pingpong table); scissors

Invite people to cut out pictures of people of different sorts from the magazines. Decide which tables they would be welcome or unwelcome at and place them at the table where you think they would be most welcome. Don't glue them down, as other people might want to change the places where they'd be welcome.

Talk about anything surprising that comes up. (You might need to choose someone very wise to lead this activity.)

6. VIP GUEST BADGE

You will need: a badgemaking machine or card circles; safety pins; tape; coloured pens

Make a badge with VIP GUEST on it.

Talk about how Jesus welcomes absolutely anybody to eat with him, not just people we might think of as VIPs. In Jesus' kingdom, young people, poor people, people who lead bad lives and people who are messy are all VIPs.

7. MESSY PEOPLE

You will need: a white or light-coloured table top; paint

Squirt paint on to the table top and invite people to draw the story as you tell it from Matthew 9:9–12, drawing characters into the paint with their fingers and hands.

Talk about the way you're now really messy and need to go and wash. Jesus loved to spend time with people whose lives were really messy. By spending time with them, he showed them how they could get rid of the messy bits of their lives that held them back.

8. BIG BARRIER

You will need: junk cardboard boxes and sheets; tubes; sticky tape; string; scissors

Make a life-sized 'border control area' out of the junk, for role-play. You might include a booth for an official to sit in, a barrier that goes up and down, a screening machine, a computer to check you are who you say you are, a set of forms to fill in and be stamped—all the stuff of nightmares from airports.

Talk about the way we only let certain people, with the right qualifications, into our country, but Jesus put up no barriers at all. Anyone could come close to him, and he showed this by eating with anybody and everybody.

9. COOKING ROUND THE WORLD

You will need: food chosen by invited participants; serviettes; cutlery; plates

Invite members of your church or community from different countries to come and prepare a dish from their country or culture in front of others. Suggest something like a sauce or dip or salad, which can be compiled on a table top and doesn't mean spending hours in a kitchen.

Have the invited guests making and talking about their dishes, explaining why they are made, when they are eaten and what's in them. Let families taste small quantities (under parental supervision in case of allergies) and enjoy the variety.

Talk about how different cultures can enjoy eating together.

10. DRESSING UP

You will need: clothes for dressing up; a screened-off area set up to suggest a first-century Middle Eastern room (with low table, rugs and cushions); basic food (for example, small pieces of pitta bread); drinking water

Choose some clothes that suggest huge wealth and some that suggest great poverty, plus others that might suggest loose living of one sort or another (I leave it to your imagination).

Put your best improvisers in charge of this activity: one plays the part of Matthew, one is Jesus if you have enough leaders, and two are disapproving Pharisees. Encourage the families to dress up as people from the town and come and eat at Matthew's house. He tells everyone how he's just met this wonderful man called Jesus, who has changed his life. He wants everybody to meet Jesus too. The Pharisees make a point of criticising every sort of person who comes to eat with Jesus—their dreadful lifestyles, terrible habits and sordid pasts. (Have fun without getting personal!) Act out the Pharisees' disapproval of the company Jesus keeps, as described in Matthew 9:10–11.

CELEBRATION

STORY

Describe the setting in Jesus' culture: eating with people meant that you accepted them and were happy to be identified as one of them. The Pharisees showed how holy they were by never eating with people who weren't as 'holy' as them. Tax collectors were collaborators with the Romans and were systematically dishonest.

Bring your actors in from the dressing-up activity and ask them to act out the full story of the episode from Matthew

9:10–11. Everyone in the room can be used as the riffraff or dishonest tax collectors gathered in Matthew's house, and as Jesus' disciples. If you feel confident in hot-seating, you might hot-seat a few members of the crowd, asking them what they think of Jesus' welcome and his willingness to sit and eat with them.

Draw the story together by talking about how exciting it was for Jesus to sit and eat with people like this—but how risky it was too. It showed how much he cared about ordinary people, and it showed that they could come close to God, just as much as apparently 'holy' people could. But it meant that Jesus risked being labelled a 'sinner' too. Even so, he carried on doing it. He made it clear how much he wanted everybody to know him and to know what forgiveness means, so that they could have happier lives, closer to God.

PRAYER

Read out:

Jesus said, 'Here I am! I stand at the door and knock. If anyone hears my voice and opens the door, I will come in and eat with that person, and they with me' (Revelation 3:20).

Have someone posted at the door of the room you're meeting in, to knock loudly.

Jesus, thank you that you want to come into our lives.

Knock again.

Jesus, thank you that you wait for us to open the door to you.

Knock again.

Jesus, thank you that you want to sit and eat with us, just as we're going to do now with each other.

Knock again and keep knocking.

Jesus, thank you that you never stop knocking! Amen

SESSION 3

THE LAST SUPPER

Aim: to explore how a meal means far more than just eating together

Bible reference: Matthew 26:17–30

This session takes ten ways in which the Last Supper of Jesus is about more than just the material things eaten, drunk and used during the event. It is an exploration of symbolism in the context of thinking of the hospitality of God. What is he, as host, trying to communicate in a non-verbal way by giving us a meal as one of the central rituals of faith (for many Christians)?

As this is a more diverse theme than many, you might want to prepare a handout that each person can take round, which gives them a chance to jot down the hidden meaning of each object or action in today's story.

ACTIVITIES

1. SYMBOLISM OF A STORY FROM THE PAST (PASSOVER)

You will need: a low table set up with the different foods from a Seder meal (you can find suggestions online)

Have a 'host' welcoming people to the table and telling a shortened version of the story of the original Passover from Exodus 12, based on opportunities to sample the different foods (check allergies). See if each group can remember what all the different foods stand for after you have finished telling the story.

2. SYMBOL OF CUP

You will need: printouts of Bible verses as below; disposable plastic wine cups; scissors; glue; red tissue paper

Go to www.biblegateway.com and do a search on 'cup' in an easy-to-read Bible version, then copy and paste the verses from Job through to Zechariah that include 'cup'. (The ones before this, in Genesis to Nehemiah, are less symbolic.) Print these verses out several times on paper, in bold and a small font (10pt or smaller) and either cut them into strips or let the families do this for themselves (my preferred option every time).

Invite families to decorate the outside of a wine cup with ripped strips of red tissue paper interspersed with strips of paper bearing the verses you have printed out. The print should show through the pasted tissue paper if the tissue paper is kept to one layer.

Talk about what the word 'cup' stands for in the verses they choose and look them up in context if people are puzzled or interested.

3. SYMBOL OF WINE

You will need: old wine bottles (cleaned and with labels removed); flat-bottomed glass beads; artificial leaves or good-quality paper and a leaf template to make your own; glue or glue gun; craft wire; wirecutters

A glue gun works best for this activity but it is more risky: make it a family-only activity, with the adult wielding the gun.

Decorate a wine bottle with the glass beads, giving each person no more than 15–20, to make a bunch of grapes on the side of the bottle and a leaf or two above it. Add tendrils made out of spiralled craft wire. (You can see pictures on Pinterest.com if you search 'wine bottle grapes'.)

Talk about Jesus' words: 'This is my blood of the covenant, which is poured out for many for the forgiveness of sins' (Matthew 26:28). What did he mean?

4. SYMBOL OF BREAD

You will need: really crispy crumbly small bread rolls (and gluten-free option); glue; A5 card; pens

Checking for allergies, invite people to break open the roll to eat it while you talk.

When Jesus said at the Last Supper, 'Take and eat; this is my body' (Matthew 26:26), what do you think he meant? Try to find one word that sums up what he meant. Write that word in bubble letters on the card, cover the inside of the letters with glue, and stick on the crumbs that have fallen from your roll, to fill in the words like a mosaic.

5. SYMBOL OF TABLE

You will need: wood; sandpaper; hammers; nails

Make a low makeshift table out of the wood by sanding the pieces, then nailing them together.

Talk about what happens around tables. Ask what tables people can think of from stories they've read. Ask how tables are used at home or at school. Ask what tables they use or see in church and which they like best.

6. SYMBOL OF FOOTWASHING

You will need: a huge picture or model (the bigger the better) of feet in sandals; paint; paintbrushes; floor covering

Use brushes to flick paint at the feet. Cover them in paint.

Talk about how, in Jesus' time, travellers got very dirty feet. When they came to a house for a meal, a slave would have the unpleasant job of washing their feet as part of the welcome. Imagine what they might have trodden in! Jesus took on the slave's job—but not just to get his disciples' feet clean. Why else do you think he washed their feet? What was he trying to show them?

7. SYMBOL OF LOVE

You will need: halved grapes; edible long thin sticks, either savoury (healthier) or sweet; an icing bag with a very fine nozzle filled with cream cheese; raisins; paper plates

Make an edible picture of the Last Supper, using the sticks to make the table and the grapes as Jesus' and the disciples' heads around it. Squirt on eyes and beards in cream cheese, finishing off the pupils of the eyes with raisins. Share the picture with someone you love.

Talk about the way Jesus gave his disciples a special meal to remind them always how much he loved them.

8. SYMBOL OF EQUALITY

You will need: catapults made from rubber bands and lolly sticks (search online for instructions); mini marshmallows; black Sharpie pen; a shoebox lid; paper

Mark a marshmallow with a face to represent yourself. Lay the shoebox lid down, a little way away from the launch line and catapult, over a piece of paper that says 'top' at one of the narrow ends of the lid and 'bottom' at the other. The game is to make your marshmallow 'sit' at the top of the table, in the most important place, by pinging it there on the catapult.

Talk about how some guests at meal tables sit in the most important seats so that everyone can see how special they are. At Jesus' table, though, nobody is more important than anybody else: we are all really important guests at Jesus' table and he is the only one with a 'special' place at it.

9. SYMBOL OF BROKENNESS

You will need: old wax crayons; heart-shaped ice cube mould trays; baking parchment; pen; oven set to 150°C/300°F/Gas Mark 2

People can strip the paper coverings off the wax crayons, break them into smaller pieces if desired, and pick the colours they like to put into a heart-shaped mould. Fill the mould up with pieces of crayon. Use a small piece of baking parchment to name each one.

Bake in the oven until the wax melts enough to hold the pieces together in each mould (about ten minutes). Remove from oven and allow to cool (in the fridge or freezer to speed up the process if necessary). You now have a new wax crayon.

Talk about what Jesus meant when he said that the bread was like his body being broken. Talk about how the only way for him to beat death for good was to be broken—just as the only way to get a new, very different and amazing crayon was to break up the old ones.

10. SYMBOL OF TOGETHERNESS/ COMMUNITY IDENTITY

You will need: matchboxes or small containers; airdrying clay; card; pens

Model a tiny cup and plate to go inside the container as symbols of Holy Communion. Make a cover for the container, decorated with the words 'We eat, therefore we are.'

Talk about the way food brings us together as a family and as a church. We have an identity because we eat together. Christians share meals and also share this special meal to remember Jesus and to remind themselves that we are all 'one' because of him.

CELEBRATION

STORY

What an amazing meal the Last Supper is! On the surface it looks like an ordinary meal at an ordinary table for ordinary people, with an ordinary cup and an ordinary loaf of bread. But we've been exploring today some of the secrets hidden in this meal, which turn it from an ordinary meal into an *extra*ordinary meal.

Set up the symbols one by one, inviting everyone to share what the 'hidden secrets' might be behind each symbol—the table, seating arrangements, welcome arrangements, bread, cup and wine. Tell the story of the Last Supper and, if appropriate, share the bread and wine as part of the re-enactment of the story; alternatively, do a form of Holy Communion that is appropriate within your denomination.

PRAYER

It may be appropriate simply to say the Lord's Prayer together.

SESSION 4

THE EARLY CHURCH

Aim: to see how Christians working together on hospitality can make a difference in society

Bible references: Acts 6:1–4; Acts 28:7; Romans 12:13

ACTIVITIES

1. VISITORS' BOOK

You will need: notebooks; pencils; rulers; decorations; wrapping paper; sequins and other decorations; glue; scissors; pens; labels printed with 'Visitors'

Invite everyone to make a Visitors' Book for visitors to their house to sign and leave a comment.

Use the pencil and ruler to rule each page of a notebook (or as many pages as you have time for) into three columns for name, address and comment. Decorate the cover.

Talk about the different people who come to your house, and the ways you can make them feel welcome. The first Christians loved welcoming strangers.

2. ST GEORGE'S CHURCH, BAGHDAD

You will need: prints of photos from www.frrme. org showing the work of St George's; pins or sticky tack; a prayer board

In some parts of the world, Christians can't get good jobs because they're Christians, and war can make life very difficult for everyone. St George's Church in Baghdad works very hard to provide food and shelter, education and aid for people who have lost homes and jobs in Iraq.

Pick a photo and pin it up on the prayer board. Pray for the people in the photo and for St George's, as they do such great work.

3. LOVE IS THE KEY

You will need: old keys; felt or foam hearts; Sharpie pens; glue; gold thread

Decorate your key with the materials provided. Write on it, or on the heart, 'Love is the…'

Talk about the way the love of Jesus opens the door of church, of our home and of the gate of heaven to absolutely everybody: we can all have a key.

4. PHILOXENIA PHUN

You will need: printouts of the word PHILOXENIA running down the left-hand side of the paper; pens

This funny word means 'hospitality' in ancient Greek. It's made up of two words put together: *philos* ('friend') and *xenos* ('stranger').

What is hospitality all about? Can you find a word or phrase that starts with each letter of *philoxenia*, that has something to do with hospitality and welcome?

Talk about the ways in which the early church showed hospitality—feeding needy strangers, welcoming each other to their homes, having travellers to stay and eating meals together.

5. OUR MEAL

You will need: foodstuffs collected for a foodbank, or paper plates and pens; a set of labels printed with the names of different community groups, such as your local football team, your church, your Brownie pack and your school

Eating a special meal together is a good way to show that you belong to each other. Can you put together a meal for one of these community groups that would be just right as a special meal for them? (If you don't have enough food to use, or if it's unsuitable, you could draw the meal on paper plates.)

Talk about the way the early Christians showed that they belonged together by eating a special meal of bread and wine together, as well as other, more normal meals.

6. DUVET DERBY

You will need: duvets and duvet covers; a whistle or hooter

Have a competition to see who can put a duvet cover on a duvet in the shortest time.

Talk about the sort of things you need to do to prepare for somebody coming to your house to stay.

7. LUGGAGE BOBBLE

You will need: wool in bright colours; sets of pompom 'doughnut shapes' in card; scissors

The early Christians travelled all round the Mediterranean to share the good news about Jesus with all sorts of people. Like us, they must have had luggage when they travelled.

Make a pompom to go on your suitcase or bag, to make the bag easier to spot when it comes off the plane or is sitting in a train luggage rack. Make sure you leave enough wool to tie it on by.

(You will find plenty of pompom instructions online if you are unsure how to do it. It's quite a long activity, so it is rather nice for children to start and finish it and parents to fill in the middle as they go round.)

Talk about what it must have felt like to stay in other people's houses all the time.

8. 'ACCESS ALL AREAS' LABEL

You will need: plastic name label holders on badges or lanyards (ask someone who attends a lot of conferences to save them for you); card; pens; stamper; stencils of the alphabet or stick-on letters; printout of an image search of 'access all areas'

Make an 'Access all areas' badge for yourself in an appropriately self-important style. Make sure you include a cross on the design somewhere, as that's the only way we have access to God!

Talk about the way that Christians in the early church were really different from the cultures around them: the Christians welcomed anybody, no matter how young or old, rich or poor, wherever they came from and whatever they believed.

Jesus' death on the cross meant that everybody could come close to God, not just a few holy, rich, educated, noble men from the right country.

9. WELCOME POSTER

You will need: printouts of the word 'welcome' in different languages, in large letters that can be painted; paints; brushes; large pieces of backing paper or card; glue

Paint the words for 'welcome' in bright colours and, when dry, glue them on to the backing paper to make a colourful poster to put in your church porch or on the noticeboard.

Talk about the way the early church welcomed and helped people from all sorts of countries and backgrounds, not just people who were like themselves.

10. HOME FROM HOME

You will need: a large (floor-sized) rough map of the Mediterranean region; ten open-topped cardboard boxes of different sizes, each labelled with a city that Paul or the other apostles visited or is mentioned in Acts (such as Corinth, Ephesus, Philippi, Athens, Pisidian Antioch, Syrian Antioch, Damascus, Rome, Galatia and Thessalonica); paper

Set up the map with a box in roughly the right place for each city. People should make a paper plane to represent an apostle and, standing round the edge of the map, try to make the plane land in the 'house' (or box) of a particular city.

Talk about how the inns and hotels were dangerous places in those days. Travelling Christians, like Paul or Barnabas, would need to sofa-surf in other people's houses, even if they didn't actually know their hosts.

CELEBRATION

Play a game together in a circle: have four or more 'houses' or bases marked by chairs or taped out on the floor. Give everyone a coin (this can be a cardboard token). Choose a home-owner for each house.

People tap each other gently on the shoulder. If you are tapped, you have to pass your coin over to the person tapping you. Every now and then, the leader shouts 'Bandits!' and everyone has to take refuge in one of the houses—but they can only go in if they can pay their way with a coin! Those left out in the cold suffer some dreadful fate like being tickled to death by bandits (you can invent a suitable forfeit that won't leave half your families in tears). Play the game once or twice, redistributing coins each time.

Talk about how hard it was when you had no money to find a sheltering home, and how rich the home-owners were with all those guests.

Play the game again, but this time, when the bandits come, anyone can go into a home, whether or not they have money to pay.

The first Christians really cared for the people around them who had no home or not enough to eat. They gave away their money to make sure the poor people were fed, and they opened their own homes to people who were travelling around to share the news about Jesus. They called this 'hospitality'.

Christians today do the same: we support and run foodbanks for people who are hungry and we look after families who are homeless, even when they have no money at all. We still call it 'hospitality'—welcoming strangers in the name of Jesus. It's what Christians do, because Jesus said that whenever we do this for each other, we're actually doing it for him. It doesn't matter whether someone has a coin to pay their way or has nothing at all: Jesus welcomes everybody and so do we.

PRAYER

Put a sheet of paper or card on the floor, with treasure chests drawn on it. Label the chests (in words or pictures): 'my home', 'my money', 'my food', 'my time', 'my listening', 'my love' and any other ways you can think of for people to express hospitality.

Redistribute your coins or tokens and pray, 'Jesus, help us to use what we have to welcome other people and make them feel at home with you and with us.'

Invite everyone, as a sign of commitment, to put their 'coin' on top of the treasure chest labelled with the kind of hospitality they would like to show.

SESSION 5

THE HEAVENLY HOME

Aim: to live in the awareness of the hospitality of heaven

Bible reference: Revelation 21:9—22:5

ACTIVITIES

1. FREE PAINT

You will need: large sheets of paper; painting materials; a Bible; printed copies of Revelation 21:9—22:5

Set aside a quieter space and invite people to listen to the description of the heavenly city from Revelation 21:9—22:5, then to paint how it sounds to them. If they can read, they could have a copy of the passage to remind them of the details.

Try not to talk too much, but give people space to be quiet and think about the amazing images.

2. BUILD THE CITY WALLS AND GATES

You will need: lots of Lego; Bibles

Set out the Lego, with copies of the Bible, open at Revelation 21, available all round it. Invite people to work together to build a model of the heavenly city as described by John.

Talk about the way John is speaking in pictures—describing what the holy city is *like* rather than what it *is*. You might remind people of the session on symbols in the Last Supper, so that they can think about what the different symbols in the city might mean.

3. GLORIOUS!

You will need: squares of brightly coloured felt, roughly 5 cm square; small mirrors used in needlework; embroidery silks; needles

Sew a mirror on to the brightly coloured felt to remind you of the bright beauty of the heavenly city in John's picture. (You can find instructions online if you search for 'easy shisha embroidery'.) People can either just sew the mirror on to the felt with stitches in a star shape or they can continue and make a border all round the mirror if they have more patience.

Talk about John's vision and the way he struggles for words to say how beautiful the city is. What is your favourite city? Where would you most like to live?

4. EVERYBODY WELCOME

You will need: facepaints; brushes; water

Paint a cross on the back of someone else's hand, using the colours they prefer.

Talk about the way the heavenly city is open to everybody who loves Jesus. The angels only guard the gates to keep out those who don't love Jesus. Anyone is welcome who has been forgiven of all the bad things they've done, through Jesus' death on the cross: it doesn't matter who they are or what they've done. Even the thief on the cross next to Jesus could go in!

5. LIGHT!

You will need: glow-in-the-dark paint; vinegar; bicarbonate of soda; containers; a dark space; a tray or a means of clearing up

Mix the vinegar and paint together and add them to the bicarb in the container. Watch the mixture effervesce up in a glowing explosion. Try adding different coloured paints to either the vinegar or the bicarb and see what happens.

Talk about the wow factor of the colours, and how John is trying to catch the wow factor of the beautiful, brightly

181

coloured city, which doesn't need the sun or moon to light it. God wants to welcome us all to this city.

6. AMAZING TREES

You will need: paper or card; scissors; pencils; masking tape; paints; rollers; sequins or craft jewels; glue

Fold the paper in half and draw the trunk and branches of half a tree on to one side, with the centre fold going up the centre of the trunk and foliage. Keeping the paper folded, cut out the shape and open it up to make a whole tree.

Either hold the tree stencil in place or tape it down on to a second piece of paper with small pieces of masking tape. Roll over it with different coloured paints, then remove the stencil and allow the paint to dry. Glue on sequins or jewels to represent fruit.

Talk about the trees that John saw standing next to the river in the city. Which part of the description of the trees do you like best? Are you more at home in the countryside or in the city? In this heavenly city there seems to be a lot of countryside too!

7. STREET OF GOLD

You will need: wallpaper sample books; paint sample leaflets; old colour magazines; used gold wrapping paper or similar; either a hexagon paper punch or templates; pencils; scissors; glue; a long narrow piece of card

Make hexagons out of gold paper. Glue the backs and make a patchwork street of hexagonal 'paving stones' along the backing card. You could do this as a joint project or make individual pictures.

Talk about the golden main street of the city of God that John describes. Imagine being invited to a place where the very street is made of gold! Have you ever been invited anywhere that is simply amazing? Would you have liked to live there always?

8. BOUND CLOSE

You will need: lengths of thick cord or rope; someone who can tie knots

Learn how to tie a knot. You could practise any simple basic knot or, if you want something with extra meaning, tie a Celtic heart knot (find tutorials online). Some people may prefer to play at three-legged races by tying their legs together.

Talk about the way knots bind things together. John describes the closeness of God to his people, in the city that is their home, and we are close to God even now if we choose to be. St Patrick wrote a prayer in which he said, 'I bind unto myself this day the strong name of the Trinity'—reminding himself how close God was to him.

9. PEARL GATES

You will need: card; pencils; very small pearl beads; glue; printouts of Philippians 3:20 in *THE MESSAGE* version: 'We're citizens of high heaven!'

Decorate the border of the printed verse with pearly beads in a zigzag, swirly or other design. Draw the design with pencil first, then squirt glue over the lines and drop beads on to the glue. The pearl beads remind us of the pearl gates of the city.

Talk about the way Christians know that we are only in our homes on earth for a short time, and our real home is close to God in heaven.

10. BIG CITY

You will need: atlases; rulers; a display board; a pen

John describes the city in his vision as being 12,000 stadia in length and width. That's about 1400 miles along each side. Use the atlas to measure how big that is and write it on the display board in terms people can understand—for example, it's about as far as London to Lisbon.

Talk about how the city is big enough for everyone. God longs to have as many people as possible at home in heaven, happy with him, not just a handful.

CELEBRATION

STORY

You might like to display some slides with pictures of different homes while you tell this story.

'Where is my home?' asked John on his island. 'Is home here where I'm living? I live in a house here, but it's not where I want to live. Perhaps my home is where I was born? But I moved away from there a long time ago. Perhaps my home is where my family is? But the people I love live all over the place! Which home would be mine?'

John thought and thought about home, and wondered and wondered where his home really was. 'Where do I really belong?' he thought. 'Where am I safe? Where can I be "me"? Where can I relax with people I love around me? Where can I welcome other people and make them feel at home too?' None of the places he thought of were ever quite right. They were lovely homes but not... not the best home... He wanted a home that would be the best place ever, with the best people ever, where he could welcome in more and more and more people to enjoy it.

Then John had a dream, or perhaps a vision. In the vision he saw the home that God had got ready for him. He saw a beautiful, brightly coloured city, as crazily shiny and multicoloured and beautiful as the wildest street party or festival. He saw streets that shone like gold, and a sparkling river with amazing trees growing beside it, laden with fruit. The gates stood wide open for all the different people running in, waving at the angels on the gates. And through the streets of the city danced the king, spinning and waltzing and breakdancing with the people, shouting, 'Welcome! You are all welcome! My son has paid the price and now you can

185

all come in!' John knew that this was the perfect home for him, with no goodbyes, just endless hellos, as people streamed in to join the party with no end.

When he woke up, the dream stayed with him, and he lived the rest of his life knowing that one day he would be running through the gates of that city into the best home, with the best people and the best person ever waiting for him.

PRAYER

Make a house shape out of everybody in the room by having them all standing in a square, with their arms up to make a roof. (Some people will inevitably crawl or run inside it.) Invite people to add their own details to the spaces in the following prayer.

As you face inwards, pray, 'Lord Jesus, thank you for our homes here on earth that give us […].'

Now face outwards: 'Lord Jesus, help us to welcome everybody who needs a home, and thank you for organisations that work with the hungry, the homeless and refugees. We pray especially for […].'

Now turn inwards again and reform the house: 'And Lord, thank you for your welcome to the best home ever. Help us to make our homes on earth more like your home in heaven. Amen'

CONCLUSION

NOT SHUTTING THE DOOR BUT OPENING IT

This is by no means the final word on the tantalisingly challenging subject that is hospitality. What a journey! We've paused to see how hospitality encapsulates the very nature and mission of God and how hospitality, even though it's costly, brings blessing. We've scanned the marvellous way Jesus models for us what it means to be both gracious host and humble guest (and a very uncomfortable guest, too). We've galloped through the imaginative ways we can express even more hospitality in every zone of our Messy Church. We've thought about the Messy team itself and ways to express God's hospitality to each other. We've looked at ways to encourage that spirit of hospitality to bubble out into homes and workplaces from the wellspring that is the gathered once-a-month Messy Church. We've taken a leaf out of the book of the hospitality industry, looked at boundaries and safety, and tried to root it all in typical Messy Church style by exploring five different aspects of hospitality through actual Messy Church sessions and experiences.

As I opened up my computer this morning, a sad email was waiting, announcing the end of a particularly thriving and successful Messy Church. Nobody can be found to run it, now that the current leaders' circumstances have changed and they no longer have time. 'There is no one to take on this role,' it says on the church's website. Prayerfully, they have finished this ministry.

What an outcry there would have been if the same church had suggested closing down their Sunday morning gathering! What a threat to their identity and purpose as a church! What protests there would have been, what distress! How many more words would have been written on the website, explaining and justifying such an enormous step! Yet the Messy Church that was attracting more families than they could easily fit in the building once a month has been closed with two and a half lines of explanation.

What does this have to do with hospitality? I think it (scarily) highlights a challenge to the established church to consider its priorities. Of course we say we want to welcome outsiders, but do we *really* want to welcome the stranger, the sojourner and the spiritual traveller? Do we really want to bless them in the time they have with us, and do we expect to be blessed by them? Or are we actually, when it comes to the crunch, only interested in running a church gathering for people who are already part of the family? People who are already members of the club, who have signed up to the rules and can be relied on to pay the membership fee? People who are born into it and know the unwritten rules? Is our welcome to the outsider (who takes an enormous risk in coming through our doors) so fragile and insignificant to us that we can view the closing of a congregation like that Messy Church with equanimity—even, perhaps, with relief? We can return to our safe household ways, focusing entirely on the needs of those who pull their weight in making the household tick. It is still a lot of work! How can we possibly open our resources to anyone not actually signed up on our planned giving scheme?

I exaggerate for effect. And yet I despair, too, because it's not so far removed from what I see in all the denominations we work with. Church needs to change. Hospitality is the key.

I dream of a church that is inside out, whose discipleship is marked by its members' growing generosity. It learns by doing and reflecting; it receives through giving. Its open doors are so wide that the walls hardly exist, except to hold up a sheltering roof. Its mindset is shaped and its very furniture is designed with the least able, those with the least voice, the oldest and the youngest, always to the fore. Its leaders wash feet and dishes more often than they preach or play guitars or organs. Its members fight to put the needs of others before their own—not just once in a while, at special outreach events, but time after time after time, until it's such a habit that it becomes a way of life that rubs off on the generations who are older and younger than they are.

In this church, the kitchen is as important as the chapel, and the dining table doubles as the table that holds the bread and wine. Guest and host sit and feast together in laughter and tears, babies and great-grandads sitting with teenagers and the middle-aged. Single people and people in relationships of all kinds are made mind-blowingly, wholesomely, awesomely welcome, accepted just as they are, because what matters to this church is not 'Who's in and who's out?' but 'Who wants to know Christ?' Dialogue over the table, among people who are no longer enemies but guests, brings greater understanding to both sides. The community around each church member is being transformed into a tiny mirror of the home we look forward to, after we have gone through the wide door of death.

I dream of a church with hospitality in the heart and on the face of every member.

BIBLIOGRAPHY

- Jeremy M. Sorbie, 'Can reverse hospitality be effective in Christian mission today?' (2012): www.churcharmy.org.uk/Articles/413134/Our_work/Research/SCOLER/SCOLER_Library/Can_Reverse_Hospitality.aspx

- C.D. Pohl, *Making Room* (Eerdmans, 1999)

- Michael Frost, *Exiles: Living missionally in a post-Christian culture* (Baker Books, 2006)

- Ian Mobsby and Mark Berry, *A New Monastic Handbook* (Canterbury Press, 2014)

- Kenneth Tanner and Christopher A. Hall (eds), *Ancient & Postmodern Christianity: Paleo-orthodoxy in the 21st century* (IVP, 2002): https://books.google.co.uk/books?id=1kDu05KZ2cQC&dq=21st+century+christian+hospitality&source=gbs_navlinks_s

- Michael G. Cartwright, *Exploring Christian Mission Beyond Christendom: United Methodist perspectives* (University Press, 2010)

- Ian Paul's blog: www.psephizo.com

- Thom and Joani Shultz, *Why Nobody Wants to Go to Church Anymore* (Group Publishing, 2013)

- 'A good host makes the best leader': www.forbes.com/sites/robasghar/2014/08/05/a-good-host-makes-the-best-leader

- Kenneth E. Bailey, *The Good Shepherd* (SPCK, 2015)

- Karen Wilk, *Don't Invite Them to Church: Moving from a come and see to a go and be church* (Faith Alive, 2010)

- Jenny and Justin Duckworth, *Against the Tide, Towards the Kingdom* (New Monastic Library, 2011)

- James J. Fox, 'Eating: The consumption of food as practical symbol and symbolic practice', in *Remaining Karen: A study of cultural reproduction and the maintenance of identity*: http://press.anu.edu.au/anthropology/karen/mobile_devices/ch04s04.html

- Danny Meyer, *Setting the Table* (Harper Perennial, 2008)

- *State of the Nation Report 2013*: www.people1st.co.uk/getattachment/Research-policy/Research-reports/State-of-the-Nation-Hospitality-Tourism/Executive-summary-hospitality-and-tourism.pdf.aspx

- http://restaurantschools.com/resources/top-10-qualities-of-a-great-hospitality-employee

- Good Hospitality Services: http://goodhsi.com

- Henri J.M. Nouwen, *Reaching Out: The three movements of the spiritual life* (Bantam Doubleday Dell, 2000)

- Tertullian, 'The prescriptions against the heretics' (c. AD200)

- Aristedes, *Apology*, Chapter 15 (c. AD125)

- Amy Oden, 'God's household of grace' in Kenneth Tanner and Christopher A. Hall (eds), *Ancient and Post-Modern Christianity: Paleo-orthodoxy in the 21st century* (IVP, 2002)

- Monastery of the Ascension: www.idahomonks.org/sect809.htm

- Mary Gray-Reeves and Michael Perham, *The Hospitality of God* (SPCK, 2011)